Walk

Walk

A Southbound Descent Over Land from Los Angeles to
Tierra del Fuego

Dave Paco

Walk :
A Southbound Descent Over Land
From Los Angeles to Tierra del Fuego

Words, art, layout, and design by Dave Paco
Concept by j.frede
Text tightened up by Milton Rouse

Third edition, March 2017
Published by Paco Garden Enterprises
San Diego, CA
(Originally published in partnership with Frederick
Publishing, Los Angeles 2009/2010)

ISBN: 978-0-9824008-0-7

10 9 8 7 6 5 4 3 2

www.davepaco.com

To my family who put up with my wanderings.

...and a special thanks to everyone who fed me, clothed me, and sheltered me these past couple of years. It's been great to be a part of your lives and you're always welcome in mine.

My heart is shattered and scattered across the globe. Its lonely pieces connected by frail veins of asphalt, cracked and bruised. My blood is thinned by the rain and the daylight hurts my eyes. I travel by night and call nowhere my home. Sweet sister, lay me down to feel the highway's caress.

Introduction

The title of this book is not meant to deceive. I didn't walk the length of Latin America. Not even a sizeable part of it, really. Nothing that could honestly be accounted for on a general map. No, the term "walk" as I intend it to be used here serves to describe a style of travel. To go on a "walk about," or maybe "stop and smell the flowers" -- to let yourself be guided by the wind, take in your surroundings, and get to know the people and places you visit rather than rush through the experience nailed to a rigid itinerary. Live it. Walk it. Feel it.

When I decided to take a trip south I knew I wanted to do it over land. I wanted to watch the landscapes and climate change… to watch one culture melt into another… to see the people, their customs, and traditions bleed through the borders and weave themselves into one world-wide blanket across the continents.

Looking at a map, I knew I would have a long way to go but the reality of the trip didn't really sink in until J.Frede dropped me off in San Diego and I strolled over the bridge into Tijuana with my little school backpack, beat-up world atlas, and a handful of Spanish words. It became quickly apparent that this would be a hefty adventure for a strict vegetarian with little knowledge of the language or customs of the 16 countries I would eventually pass through before the trip came to an end.

At the time I left I hadn't put a whole lot of thought into my little walk about. Some ideas, some sites or cities, but mostly just the direction. With minimal supplies and minimal plan I would continue south 'til the end. This would leave me free to follow my heart or the suggestions of others or to grab on to any wild, strange opportunity that came my way. I was confident from the experiences of prior travels that even for the lack of knowledge I then possessed, I was in for an amazing, enigmatic, challenging, almost inexpressible time. I was stepping into an atmosphere so far removed from that of the "first world" where the streets are littered with trash, a thick, deadly smog defiles the air, neighborhoods are built from cinderblocks and sheets of corrugated tin, and all around seethes excessive poverty, corruption, crowds, chaos, unruly traffic, and violent crime. Through all these unsettling conditions, however, I found, more than anything else, an abundance of generosity, hospitality, friendship, and happiness.

My journey was one of growth and learning. Equally inspirational and depressing. Full of uneasy, trying moments as well as those of uncontrollable joy and awe. I made more friends than I could ever count and saw more of the world than I ever thought existed.

You hold in your hands now a collection of emails I sent back periodically to friends and family during my trip. Some grammar and awkward segments have been treated, but more or less the text has been left raw to reflect the progression of my involvement with the writing and eventual burn out of my wandering spirit. I've also included at the beginning of each chapter some snippets from my personal journal. Although I could never completely convey the immensity of my time on the road I hope you enjoy this account and that it inspires you to take on some travel of your own.

Until next time,

Dave

// ate at a little mom and pop shack // underneath it is the old prison // watched the sun set from atop a big hill // going to bed hungry again // didn't connect in time for the train // Wal-Mart in every city... the American infection is spreading // breath of fresh air // managed to get lost in the forest // hit with a torrential downpour and anything that had previously resembled a path was now a river // in the dorm room sawing logs the entire night // kept me awake buzzing in my ear and sucking my blood // gave me a headache, but I learned a lot // stairways and inclines that would give San Francisco a run for it's money // through a series of random and wrong turns stumbled upon a remarkable church // stopped and watched a couple songs and some dancing // laughed at my horrible Spanish // we laughed and danced and sang // cut and divided by stairways // like a painting I've never seen before but have always loved // back in the big city with the stench and the filth // into the "Mr. Coyote" discothèque // all hell would've broken loose // rather walk around aimlessly than think about what I'm supposed to be taking pictures of // high school punker party // to drink an old bottle of wine stamped 1802 and the "Kingdom of Napoleon" // ripped off by the bus driver // I really should never go against my intuition // life, for me, is a broken heart // cold blade of the knife // good night, little book //

From: **Paco Paco** (pacogardenrecords@hotmail.com)
Sent: Thu 9/14/06 4:13 PM
To: **All Friends** (amigos@everywhere.com)
Subject: **Southbound.**

Friends and Family, Brothers and Sisters…

Writing to you now the first report on my journey south into Latin America. About two weeks ago I entered Mexico by way of Tijuana and cut east through baked, barren desert wastelands to Mexicali and there turned south to Hermosillo and then on to Los Mochis. Visually, the first couple days felt very similar to any other in a small town of Southern California or Western Texas. As I continued further the desert landscape began to sprout occasional lone, tall cacti and I felt like I was in an old western film. Culturally, however, I was out of my element. I walked out of the U.S. with a handful of Spanish words like, "Hola. Gracias. Por Favor. Como te llamas? Queso. Frijoles. Uno, Dos, Tres…" This rudimentary basis of the language really did nothing to help me find cheap hotel rooms, vegetarian food, or directions to bus terminals, etcetera. I was lost. Thankfully my friend Dulce had entrusted me with her little Spanish/English pocket dictionary and I quickly constructed vocabulary lists of the words and phrases that seemed most necessary in my day-to-day struggles to get by. Since I learned to ask, "Como se dice," I've been molesting everyone I can in the street, on buses, and in the plazas to learn more words and how to grammatically use them to my benefit. I've been lucky to cross paths with so many patient people.

At Los Mochis I caught the Chihuahua Pacific train heading up Barranca del Cobre (Copper Canyon). We started off slow, cruising through the corrugated metal shacks that make up the shantytowns surrounding the city and eventually picked up speed and pushed towards the canyon, calmly swallowed by amassing greenery. The lush, leafy landscape, still moist from last night's rain began to bubble up into hills rolling larger and larger as we crept close to them. As we entered their terrain we, too, began our ascent. Side by side with the river we glided slowly towards the clouds. The vivid plant life around us was interrupted only here and again with flowering cacti the size of small trees and next came the trees themselves. I felt I had wandered into another time. As if at any moment I might catch a glimpse of brontosaurus or a pterodactyl or some other odd amphibious dinosaur crawling out of the water below. And this other, lost time slowly morphed into a fairy tale land as, mile after mile, butterflies of every shape, size, and color fluttered about the train. On we pushed. In and out of tunnels and past occasional trash and scattered bones. The 'little engine that could' roared into the canyon, into this beautiful abyss and carried us onward toward the heavens. Finally, as we gained some altitude great rocks broke through the hillsides and the greenery seceded like dress straps falling from a woman's shoulders. And then, all at once, we overcame it. We soared above the clouds to look down at this breath-taking gash in the land below.

Deeper than the Grand Canyon and be-speckled with the colorful Tamahumaran people, Barranca del Cobre is a mighty sight to see. We made our way through San Rafael to the small town of Creel where I got off to take a room for the night. I had hoped to visit the old mining town of Batopilas nearby and hike down into the canyon for a day or two but some wicked rain kicked up and didn't seem likely to quit. The buses to Batopilas were quite infrequent as well so I just hung out and toured around Creel on a bicycle. I made a few friends there and left with them to the city of Chihuahua.

Rossana and her daughter Rebeca put me up for a couple nights in Chihuahua. I walked about the city during the days to check out the many historical sites, churches, and markets but never did find the damn vegetarian restaurant people kept telling me about. Eating has been a little difficult but as my vocabulary improves and I learn how to construct the sentences I mean to ask it gets better. Rice and beans are almost always available. And I did find a little joint on a lonely side street back in Hermosillo that serves vegetarian chorizo. I'll get by. However, Mexico is economically more stressful to my wallet than either India or Thailand was, at least here in the north. Between food, lodging, and transportation I'll probably blow my finances much more quickly than I had anticipated and will have to cut the trip short. I'll have to shave off some less important destinations if I want to make it to the others. Considering, I dropped straight south from Chihuahua to Zacatecas.

Arriving at night the city was faintly illuminated by neon crosses above the churches and on the hilltops like those you'd see over a homeless shelter. In the morning I looked out over twisting, turning, narrow cobblestone streets and multi-pastel colored cement block houses strewn randomly across the hillsides like confetti. Around every corner I'd find an ancient church or historical site of some sort -- the "Colonial Mexico" you hear about in travel books. I took in as much as I could of this cultural heritage and then met some kids who were intent on dragging me to parties all over the city. We danced all night and hid from the heavy rains in the afternoons.

Leaving Zacatecas I caught a ride in the back of a pick-up truck halfway to the megalopolis of Guadalajara. I rode the rest of the way in on a soda pop delivery truck, took a cheap room in the red light district and spent a few days wandering around the huge city by foot. Some punk rockers gave me a flyer for a show and I met some new friends there who put me up for a couple nights and showed me everything I'd missed in the city so far.

Next I cut over to the old colonial town of Guanajuato, a highly romantic city with more cobblestone, hills, history, and a honeycomb network of traffic tunnels beneath the city. A very pretty place, but all the cutesy touristy couples made me queasy so I ran east to San Miguel de Allende... even more touristy.

I write to you now from San Miguel, perched some three hundred kilometers or so north of Mexico City where I'm waiting 'til morning to drop down into the big city for the September 16th Independence Day super-fiesta. I look forward to Mexico City, land of the Aztecs, most populous city in the world... it's a little intimidating. The scenery so far has been increasingly breath taking. The deserts erode into rolling hills... forest not unlike those of the Rocky Mountains... big cities, small towns... historic stone intertwined with urban cement... kind, smiling faces... and occasional good food.

That's all for now...

Love, Dave.

// we hit a dog on the highway // make their own vinegar from fermented fruits and vegetables // part of the flag caught on fire // watched the parade of military might // it rained on us and it was fun // couldn't read, stand, or think anymore // like a kid in a candy store with that goddamn camera, man // packed with lovely artifacts // so many skulls // ancient ruins side by side with the modern hustle of Mexico's markets // gory, bloody Jesus // vendors and police engaged in their dance of apprehension // voodoo and witchcraft stuff // good break dancers // told us we were angels // realized I was caught in a sliver between two worlds when, from atop the Pyramid of the Sun, some guy's cell phone started ringing // would've loved to see it back in the 30's // inspired at the art museum // wild lightning in the sky // goth/punk/metal market // the heat and electricity // burns just below the surface // people pulling their hair and jumping up and down // art is hard // line between passion and practicality // the other was horribly painful // bull fighter museum turned bar // shot bb guns in the Alameda // dirty dirty // pretty damn liberating, really // feel slightly useless // death and ritual. Burial rites // spent some time yesterday with a couple Nepalese refugees // beautiful. And sparse... almost animalistic //commandeered fleet from Oaxaca // nothing more than a game of chess once you know what you want//

From: **Paco Paco** (pacogardenrecords@hotmail.com)
Sent: Thu 10/13/06 11:48 PM
To: **All Friends** (amigos@everywhere.com)
Subject: **Mexico City.**

Friends and Family, Brothers and Sisters,

I've been about a month here in Mexico City. Didn't plan on staying so long, but it's easy to get comfortable in such a fine place. On any corner you can find fresh fruit, nuts, food, and juice alongside clothes, music, movies, books, or boots... anything you need or anything you can think of for a fraction of the price in the States. Subway travel costs about twenty cents and there are enough museums, historical sites and events to keep you busy for months on end. Although much of the city closes early there's always something to do or look at from green VW beetle taxis, towering skyscrapers, colonial masterpiece architecture, sinking churches, ornate interiors, relaxing parks, thundering markets, constant sirens... This city screams life in a language you can't ignore.

I've been staying at the Casa de los Amigos, a Quaker establishment housed in the old home and studio of the great Mexican painter and muralist Jose Clemente Orozco, whose work often appears next to that of Diego Rivera or David Alfaro Siqueiros. From Sunday potlucks to Mexican Movie Night and occasional group outings I can say I've had a very fine time here at the casa... and made so many great friends from so many places it will be hard to leave.

I rolled into town on the eve of independence, right on time for the celebrations. Just before midnight hundreds of thousands of people gathered in the Zocalo (main square and in this case believed by the ancient Aztecs to be the center of the universe) to participate in the reciting of "El Grito" -- Miguel Hidalgo's cry for independence on the dawn of revolution. The governor of the federal district delivered the Grito and, with flags waving and fists pumping, the crowd cheered him on. "Viva México!" "Viva!" "Viva Independencia!" "Viva!" The amplified voice along with the refrain from the crowd tumbled in echoes throughout the square, bouncing off the National Palace, the Metropolitan Cathedral, and even the ruins of the Aztec pyramid of Tenochtitlan. Afterwards a seemingly endless fireworks display danced in the sky above us and occasionally dropped lit shrapnel into the crowd or ricocheted off the cathedral towers. Much fun was had by everyone.

I saw the Zocalo packed with people on a few more occasions such as the arrival of teachers and supporters marching in protest almost 300 miles from Oaxaca City, where political strife has thrown the city into civil unrest, or the march commemorating the student massacre of '68 in Tlateloco. However no event was so well attended as the National Democratic Convention, which drew over one million people to the city center. Pouring out from the Zocalo into the side streets like water surrounding a clogged drain this human mass pulsed with anger, excitement and anticipation; seething at the seams and ready at any moment to boil over into the hopes and dreams of a new

16

and powerful Mexico. Shaken by a million voices calling for change I couldn't help but think that the people here and everywhere already have everything they need... they're only waiting for a leader to show them how to use it. Unfortunately, so many of our leaders are corrupt and deceitful (and solve problems with childish and asinine solutions like "building walls") so this cycle of misery will continue until the people decide to educate themselves and make the necessary changes on their own. I'm constantly amazed by Latin America's relationship with revolution and passion for equality and human rights. I guess it would be slightly difficult for an outsider to comprehend... coming from a nation with an over abundance of wealth and a tendency to waste.

The Casa de los Amigos is located here in the Tabacalera neighborhood, sandwiched in-between streets whose names, in English, would read 'Insurgents' and 'Reform' and an equal distance from the Revolution Monument and subway stop of the same name. I've been painting the hallways here in exchange for a free bed in the dormitory. I've also just completed another job painting a house for some cash. I spend most afternoons volunteering at a safe house for homeless kids giving drawing lessons or playing games. The yogi who runs the joint is a vegetarian monk from the Philippines and all meals fall into accord. The youngsters who attend Casa Ananda aren't quite as enthused by the vegetarian food as I, but they deal with it. I've been impressed, actually, by the amount of vegetarian food I've found in Mexico City. There's a

Hare Krishna restaurant around the corner and a grocery store called "Super Soya" just down the street from that. Most kids at the Casa Ananda are fifteen to twenty years old, making an attempt to get off drugs, off the streets, and into school or work of some kind. The house acts as a launch pad for them. It's sad to see so much talent and potential sitting idle in such sweet kids, but I enjoy spending time there. I only wish my Spanish was better so I could hold real conversations with them. Maybe I'll return…

Next I'm heading east to Puebla, to Veracruz, and then south again. Hope all is well with you all wherever you are.

Love, Dave

P.S.- Happy Friday the 13th!

(some) MEXICO CITY HIGHLIGHTS:

1. Mechanical Bull (enough said).
2. Lucha Libre (Mexican Wrestling... amazing acrobatics under the guise of good and evil)
3. Museum of Archaeology / Museum of National Art
4. Teotihuacan (pre-Aztec ruins... Two miles down the Avenue of the Dead to the stunning Pyramids of the Sun and Moon)
5. Salsa Lessons (hell of a good time, but I need a few more)
6. Soccer Game (America vs. Monterrey at the colossal 100,000+ Estadio Azteca [stadium])

// not an ounce of respect // got drunk on vodka and mezcal // her body writhed demonically // I'm excited to sleep // oh, humidity, how do I hate thee // wet, sticky rubber // the volcano it sits beneath // smells of exhaust and sewage and is generally ugly // the water felt fucking great // wasn't a damn thing to eat except McDonald's and Burger King // saw some BMX freestyle bikers // turned out to be an ordeal // lost in strange mountain towns // spent most of the time teasing me // only peace between them // bought me water and a popsicle // traded funny hand tricks // arrive around 4:00 in the morning with nothing to do // live and learn… again and again // looked like a war zone // ate a couple of pastries and passed out // haunted by the ghost of a mosquito // over 2000 year old tree // use the de-wheeled vehicles as land marks // scenic views and small towns // dog eating a coconut // made a skull in the sand // trash and attitude // live in a cave // rocky trail with my bare feet and saw a long snake // shake up the shore // saw a school of fish in a wall of water // ate peanuts in my hammock and listened to the waves // feel very disconnected today // bites of all different kinds of insects all over // so much salt water slammed up my nose // Latin black // went to the turtle museum // on the black sand beaches of Mermejita under a fiery red sunset sky // stars and crescent moon took over the night sky // weak and dizzy // can't expect anything // FTW // in another place mentally // with the dirty dogs and their fleas // fighting against the mist and haze that hung sleepily to the coast // broke from a pale orange smudge to a bright, fiery disc // I love being awake in the morning // a lot of nudists here // today I'm into magic and connection // waiting and waiting and waiting //

From: **Paco Paco** (pacogardenrecords@hotmail.com)
Sent: Tue 10/31/06 3:15 PM
To: **All Friends** (amigos@everywhere.com)
Subject: **Oaxaca at War vs. The Calm of the Coast.**

Friends and family, brothers and sisters...

First and foremost, Happy Halloween! Hope it's been creepy. I'm writing from the little town of Chiapa de Corzo in the state of Chiapas, Mexico. After a grueling two days that tried my patience with the lost art of hitchhiking I finally tumbled into town. I'll spend Dia de los Muertos here or in nearby San Cristobal de las Casas. Already the candy skulls and colorful decorations line the markets and you know I'm excited!

After a short stroll through the markets of Puebla and a dip in the Gulf of Mexico at Veracruz I turned south to the city of Oaxaca. Since early summer the city has been victim to political strife and a whirlwind of power struggles. The Oaxaca Teachers Union has been on strike in demand of practical wages and school supplies, but an order was given to attack striking teachers in the city center by the governor Ulises Ruiz. Police tear-gassed the citizens who turned to forcefully push the police out and barricade the streets to keep them from re-entering. Using city buses, cars, cement, barbed wire, steel, and anything else on hand they closed off a good portion of central Oaxaca and kept watch with sticks and Molotov cocktails. Eventually the police backed off and the people were left in a fury, but in control of the city and government

21

offices. The movement that started with the teachers has now grown into a major political push to remove Ruiz from office and overhaul the system in general.

When I arrived early in the dark of morning a couple weeks ago, the city was covered in spray-paint and many roadblocks still stood, illuminated by smoldering fires and surrounded by rubble. Police and military had been absent for about six months. Most everything was functioning normally without them. Graffiti everywhere in site read "Ulises out of Oaxaca" or "Rat, liar, murderer," etc. By this time it was hard to tell where there was an actual movement and where people were looking for an excuse to shout a little bit or write on a wall. I stayed for a few days, undisturbed, and then left for the beach. Just in time, it seems, as now the military has returned in hopes to forcefully regain the city. There have been some deaths including an American journalist.

The beach in Veracruz was uncomfortably hot and humid and I was very pleased to reach the southern Oaxacan coast and find the weather just right. Puerto Escondido was a little too crowded so I slid down the shore to Mazunte. Just what I was looking for. Quiet, tranquil beaches... perfect water. People here and there, but nowhere a crowd. I bought a hammock and paid a couple bucks to hang it up at a little beach shack and use their facilities. Couldn't be happier except for the mosquitoes and sand flies! Spent my birthday lazing about on the sand or splashing in the clear blue water and explosive waves. I even traded some work on a wood-waterproofing project in exchange for my hammock space and breakfasts. For one good solid day I was as sick as a dog with what a couple locals feared might be dengue fever. I'm still not sure whether it was or not. For about a week or so I took it easy in Mazunte making friends, reading, thinking and enjoying the sea and scenery. But as all good things come to an end, I felt it was time to move on and I wanted to float this direction for Day of the Dead. I made a couple more beach stops on the coast and then... back east into Chiapas.

Thank you all so much for the mail and birthday wishes! So great to hear from everyone. Please excuse my short replies, but it's all I could afford. I'll send more pictures when I reach the Yucatan. Until then...

Love, Dave.

// the air thick with incense // left a cute and clever Gypsy-eyed girl back on the coast // the smell of mortality taints the air and that wild wind blows // tranquil river of mist, a sea of dreams // don't really care to see things or take pictures // training wheel adventure simulation shit // something to cut out the howl of the hyenas // can't wait to wash my clothes // 8 tacos and a bottle of horchata // appearing as monster extremities in the dark // rocks revealed beneath the plaster in a romantic strip-tease of time // saw so many shooting stars // pirate museum was closed // deep sleep, lots of dreams // passed the rusting corpse of a wrecked war plane // chopped weeds with machetes and sang Twisted Sister songs // went to sleep on the concrete listening to Creedence // José has grand delusions of being an Apache Indian // found a tarantula in my bed last night // gold-toothed Guatemalan cowboys with pistols in their pants and extra clips on their hips // particularly mysterious morning with fog drifting in through the jungle foliage // learning to live with mosquitoes // nursing blisters, tick bites, and spiky-plant puncture wounds // holiday blues // long day working in the rain // palm sized scorpion crawl up my neck //

From: **Paco Paco** (pacogardenrecords@hotmail.com)
Sent: Mon 12/04/06 2:24 PM
To: **All Friends** (amigos@everywhere.com)
Subject: **Tierra Maya and Life on the Farm.**

Friends and Family, Brothers and Sisters...

I hope you all had a grand Thanksgiving, ate something delicious, and put on some happy pounds. After I last wrote from Chiapas I made a whirlwind tour through the Yucatan Peninsula stopping at the ruins of many Mayan cities such as Tonina, Palenque, Chichén Itzá, Ek' Balam, and Tulúm. The most impressive of which, Palenque and Chichén Itzá, are, of course, the most popular. A visit to either is not unlike a visit to Disneyland -- swimming through the swarm of site-seers, the crowds and cameras. Magnificent structures, though. Bold, brilliant pyramids stretching their great bodies towards the heavens, telltale remains of ancient bas reliefs etched into their sides; towering white stairways standing in strong contrast to the emerald green tangles beyond; stone gods who bare their teeth, so terrifying and grotesque, as they cling to the exoskeletons of their long forgotten temples, now cold and unused. But if you squint your eyes just right you can almost imagine how the city used to look with the colorful sea of tourists flowing in and out replacing the lively markets of old.

I definitely appreciate the majesty and power of the popular sites, but enjoyed very much the serene and tranquil atmosphere of some others where once in a while I was the only one around, left alone to soak up the past in the shadows of the present. I admire the way the jungle slithers up the ruined buildings, reclaiming its stones the way it did the bodies that moved them so many years ago. It reminds me of how transitory our existence here is.

Next I took a short but refreshing break from site-seeing to share some good times and great food with very hospitable friends in the modern yet historic city of Mérida. We ate homemade sushi and Bolivian peanut soup, swam in stalactite rich underground caves, swapped vocabulary, and more.

The highway then led me back to the east coast where I made a much shorter stop at the over-priced but beautifully-beached town of Tulúm. Then south and south again where my days in Mexico came to an end at the border of Belize. However, the customs officials there only wanted to give me a two-day transit visa that I used up in Belize City. A slice right out of the Caribbean, Belize City was exciting and different. Reggae blasting out of various sound systems down all the streets and dreadlocked rastas on the corners with sweet Jamaican swagger in their speech. Most of the population is of African, Mestizo, or Asian descent and I was relieved to be speaking English again and making some sense to people. I spent my regulated days eating coconut-rich Caribbean food and talking to folks around town. I met some very fine goodhearted people in Belize and really dug the atmosphere.

I write now from Guatemala where I'm living and working on a large but lazy farm a little ways outside the town of Flores in the northern Petén Jungle. Some people have called Guatemala the gateway to Central America and I agree that it is undeniably so. As soon as we crossed the border and the highway deteriorated into rubble and dust, the jungle rose up around us, the proud trees with their fearless green fists to the sky and the air suddenly scented with magic and mystery, gun smoke and guerrilla warfare... I knew we were there.

The farm was recently bought by the Remar Foundation when the previous owner disappeared after a tax dispute with the government. It serves as a rehabilitation center for recovering drug addicts, alcoholics, and ex-cons who hope to successfully make their way back into society. I'm in the company of twenty other men including such characters as "Loco" José, Tambolis the "Hollywood Monkey," Papa Cosme "El pueblo tiene hambre," "El Tigre," "Sammy Sosa," "Mohawk" the horse, "Coffee" and "Rodeo" the bulls, "Negra" and "Momma" the dogs, and many more. I share a cinder-block room with two other guys sleeping on the shredded carcass of an old mattress laid out on the cement floor and fortified by a mosquito net. We have a little window with a couple sheets of metal for shutters, a larger sheet of metal for a door and a tin roof onto which the rain drums during the night. We work slowly from sunrise to sunset in the fields clearing grass and weeds with machetes or harvesting lemons, limes, oranges, mangos, or tamarinds. A fair amount of time is spent sitting around on the porch, eating, watching movies, or taking siestas and somehow these guys are able to, at times, stretch an hour's worth of true work throughout the entire day. The hands of many of the older men are permanently crippled to the grip of a machete handle after decades of life in the fields.

Dining on the farm is repetitive and a lifesaver for me has been the government-issued soy meat and vitamin-enriched vegetable drinks, which are distributed to the poor in Guatemala as a more economically efficient combatant against the malnutrition problem than animal derived products. But on days when those aren't available I sometimes have to settle for rice alone, although Mario, the sweet-hearted chef, always does his best to accommodate my diet in any way that he can. We walk a mile in each direction to the kitchen and back for every meal and keep a sharp eye out for vipers and jaguars in the night. The crocodiles down at the lagoon keep to themselves and not a day goes by when I don't see some type of bird or insect that I've never seen before. Life here is very relaxed. The air is clean and the grass is green. The only sounds are those of the jungle and of the songs we sing. I'm picking up a good deal of Spanish, of course, but do more listening than speaking. The Guatemalan dialect is a little different than that of Mexico. These guys speak so quickly and with so much slang that it's very difficult for me to make much sense out of what they're saying. I can stumble through a simple conversation but I'm hopeless in a group. Listening does a lot of good, though. The long strings of coded syllables slowly break apart into words and from there I can start to decipher the meanings. Many of the guys are eager to learn English and I've given a few classes already. Everything is give and get here and the more I help them the more they want to help me. At any rate, I'm told we're all brothers and family and I'm welcome to stay as long as I wish, but I've still got a long way to go and so much to see.

I don't expect to be back to a computer before the end of the month so I'd like to wish everyone Happy Holidays now!!! Stay warm up north, ha ha!

Much Love, Dave.

// I have blisters on almost all my fingers // food's been a little short lately // Sammy hit a wasps' nest today and was stung repeatedly // roof still has a leak // it's been raining for over a week // looked like hell // starving for sweet things // I've had nothing to eat but carrots, potatoes and squash for three days // hung Christmas lights up on a big tree outside // saw footprints of crocodiles and monkeys at the pond // every one here's got a sad story to tell // sweet lady with cancer in her cheek // Hanukah in the jungle // felt my feet dragging // witnessed a macho monkey fight // made a grand fire in the evening // knees hurt and I have seven blisters on my feet // can't feel my fingers // slightly distort but ultimately conform // the pavement peeling away beneath me // on Mayan Radio // she's here, but who is she? // we're very comfortable in the States... too comfortable. Taking cold-water bucket showers outside on cold nights while the highway traffic passes by makes you realize that //

From: **Paco Paco** (pacogardenrecords@hotmail.com)
Sent: Tue 1/02/07 10:44 AM
To: **All Friends** (amigos@everywhere.com)
Subject: **Lost in the Jungle… Left the Farm.**

Friends and Family, Brothers and Sisters,

Livingston, Guatemala. I arrived here by riverboat a few days ago from Rio Dulce at the other end of El Golfete ("little gulf") on the shores of Lake Izabal, the largest in Guatemala. I left the farm just after Christmas as, after five weeks, the novelty of breaking my back all day working in exchange for a dirty, lumpy bed and halfway decent food had finally worn off. The boys and I spent Christmas Eve at the cinder block church in town. After literally hours of speeches and sermons we were served a communal dinner (which consisted of tortillas and juice for me) and then the party really began. Bags and bags of fireworks were dumped into the courtyard and at midnight the entire town erupted in a bubbling frenzy as fireworks exploded in every direction. The streets became a psychedelic war zone as motorists swerved through sparks and smoke and children as well as grandparents laughed and gasped as they took turns lighting the fuses on surprise explosives. "The Body of Christ" church by this time was nothing more than a chaotic rampage as kids swung sticks in reckless abandon at a super-sized clown piñata in the midst of firework bangs, hisses, and deafening grenades. I ducked and dove to avoid being hit along with all the other folks in the yard. Happy birthday, Jesus.

Many times at the farm I couldn't help but feel as if I was on the movie set of the Latin sequel to "Cool Hand Luke" or any Vietnam War movie. I had the overall feeling when I left that I had just completed a prison sentence and indulged in sweet foods and juice all throughout town in giddy celebration. I don't yet miss the sickly green paint on the walls or the none-too-pleasant fluorescent lights but I had a difficult time saying farewell to the friends I had made there and a few tears were shed on both sides. At the farm live parts of Guatemalan life that I'll never forget like making belts and shoelaces from plastic bags, sewing pieces of used car tires to the soles of worn out shoes to keep out the water, or old Alfredo with his one good eye, crooked fingers, and scalp infection sporting so proudly his women's jacket that was the best of the bunch on donation day. So, after a time of watching some of the other guys lose control and disappear back into the streets in search of a glass pipe or a bottle, I, too, walked away from the farm, but my journey would take me deeper into the jungle in search of the ancient Maya city of "El Mirador."

Back in Flores I rounded up a small group of other foreigners to help split the price of hiring a guide and pack horses to bear the weight of supplies for our adventure into the "National Park of the Tiger." The lost city of El Mirador lies beneath dense jungle about 7 KM south of the Mexican border, which, they said, put about 75 KM between us and the ruins from our starting point in the village of Carmelita... and the only way to cover that distance is by foot. So we set off into the immense, crawling, untamed jungle through ankle to knee-deep mud, eerie swamps, kamikaze mosquitoes, treacherous spiky plants, and wild animals towards a far off goal. The journey was trying and the land rarely kind. More than once I felt that my legs wouldn't take me another step, but the only real option was to keep walking -- so we kept on. We spent the first night at El Tintal, one of the smaller, unexcavated Mayan sites we passed along the way. Here and there were signs of grave robbers who had tunneled into the ruins in search of loot. At one we found some fragments of pottery and aged Mayan bones that crumbled at the touch.

Another day of arduous trekking brought us to our destination. The site of El Mirador is believed to be the largest in the Maya world and contains the tallest pyramid, but over 90% of the site is still overgrown with jungle foliage. Archaeologists are slowly sifting through the rubble and roots but they tell me it will probably be another fifty years before the site is cleared. Instead, I used my imagination to envision what was hidden beneath the mountains of jungle growth. From the peak of "La Danta" pyramid it's not hard to imagine, though, as you look out on numerous other perfectly symmetrical mounds laid out all around and nothing else but jungle in green puffs of shag carpet rolling out uninterrupted in every direction until united with the deep blue horizon beyond. Needless to say sunrise and sunset from this point are both spectacular and surreal. Watching them I felt as if I was in a man-made planetarium and the encircling dome of celestial haze would be at any moment seized away at the end of the show. And eventually it did fade, but into another show of brilliant and unending stars sparkling above throughout the unpolluted sky. It was brought to my attention then that we were in the night of the winter solstice and exactly six years to the date away from the end of the Mayan calendar.

After a peaceful day of exploring what was to be seen of the ruins beneath the roar of the howler monkeys overhead we set off to retrace our steps back towards "civilization". At the end of five days I think we covered a total of 170 KM by foot and I can still feel it in my legs.

I spent the passing of the new year here in Livingston, the home of the famous Caribbean Garifuna culture (descendants of African slaves), but the celebrations weren't quite what I had hoped for. In the wake of some sort of money scandal, the National Bank of Guatemala has gone bankrupt and cash now is very hard to come by. The problem has driven tourists out of Guatemala and made it very difficult for locals to eat or pay bills. At midnight on New Year's Eve there was, yet again, an uproar of fireworks, but for the most part the streets were empty and the live music I had come to hear was nowhere to be found.

So now I'll head back down the river canyon and stop off at some Mayan villages and hot springs along the way in the direction of the capital and Antigua. Happy New Year one and all until next time... Love, Dave.

// rumbling thunder inside // a vision in my head // indigenous kids to smash up a piñata // pan dulce, I love you! // as soon as one is in the right place you have to adjust the second, and when that one is ready the first is out again // entwined in an ancient love // turned down a painting job in Livingston // feeding the veins // the blood thickens // the river is a world of reflection // smashed our boat directly into the other // guided the boat over a plain of glass // mañana, mañana // everything is passing… only the speed differs // we either fight the current or feel it // chased a snake out of the dining room today // a couple days of hard drinking did me in // smoked some grass with Dennis tonight // adapting to our world and not ours to theirs // fucking Valentine's Day... // a client was bitten by a vampire bat last night // little mouse trying to get at my peanuts // tourists who pass by with their little life jackets // the human race is not but a bunch of blind, bleating sheep. Help us //

From: **Paco Paco** (pacogardenrecords@hotmail.com)
Sent: Thu 2/15/07 1:38 PM
To: **All Friends** (amigos@everywhere.com)
Subject: **Finca Tatin.**

Friends and Family, Brothers and Sisters...

For the past six weeks I have been working at
the Hotel Finca Tatin, inland from Guatemala's
Caribbean Coast. I set off from Livingston ripe and
ready to get back on the road and do some traveling.
However, as the water taxi pulled up to dock at this
riverside hotel and I myself, as I walked in, was again
swallowed by the rich and rebellious jungle, glimpsing
thatch-roofed bungalows through gaps in the green
bush, I knew that I might stay longer than the one lone
night I had planned on.

The Hotel Finca Tatin, opened by Carlos
Simonini, an Italian Argentine, and the Texan house
manager, Dennis Compton (who is just a few shades shy
of Dennis Hopper), is a small operation buried in the
Guatemalan jungle on the banks of the Rio Tatin
between Livingston and Rio Dulce. I hung around here
for a couple days exploring the waterways, lagoons, and
walking trails by kayak and on foot. To the east lie the
towering walls of the Rio Dulce Canyon through which
the river twists and turns on it's way out to sea. To the
west "El Golfete," a huge expanse of water surrounded
by hills and dotted with islands, fresh water dolphins,
and manati. A precious piece of land, to say the least.
When I had seen what I'd come to see I packed my bags

to go but Dennis caught me on the way out and said, "The hotel could use an extra hand and we would gladly give you a room and three solid meals a day if you would stick around for a while." And I thought, "Well..." Hard offer to turn down in such a paradise. I had it in my mind then to remain at the Finca for another month, but that's come and gone and I still don't feel the urge to leave. Bit by bit I've been handed more and more responsibilities until now I have my hands in a piece of everything from running the reception and reservations to the money and bookkeeping, planning and alterations, internet touch-ups, artistic contribution, and occasional boat operation. Our maximum capacity stands at around forty people and we go from one or two persons to sold-out in waves.

The only way to reach the hotel is by boat and I've come to enjoy the quiet and isolation though I sometimes think of Marlon Brando in "Apocalypse Now." My heart and travel eagerness have been eased by the slow and steady current that passes by and carries students in wooden dugout canoes up and down the river to the Ak' Tenamit community project and school. Most of the surrounding population is of Q'eqchi' Mayan descent and speaks Spanish as a second language to the original native tongue. I'm trying to learn a few phrases.

I spend most of my days at the front desk, working on art projects, stretching out in a hammock with a book, or flying off the rope swing for a splash in the river and then drying off under the warm tropical sun. The water is full of fish and the land is crawling with life. Literally. If, when walking along a path, you feel yourself the victim of a thousand stares and you stop to relax your focus, you'll see that everything around you is engaged in some sort of soft and subtle shift or quick, cautious advance or retreat. Everything is moving. Armies of ants both big and small march ahead, occupied and uncaring at your feet while warrior crabs tower over them, lopsided with their one grand claw. Toucans and parrots squawk overhead and hummingbirds whiz past your ear. Snakes, spiders, and scorpions slide through the shadows. There's a four-legged rodent the size of a small dog with the head of a guinea pig and the face of a rabbit called a Cuatusa and large red lizards that run on their hind legs. Frogs and yellow swirly-eyed, clown-faced vampire flies, strange walking birds with rainbow feathers and butterflies the size of your hand... There's a little bit of everything here.

I'm told this is the dry season, but there's still a fair amount of rain from little misting showers to outright downpours that raise the river a few inches. For some time after the rain ceases to fall from the clouds it continues to drip from level to level down a labyrinth of leaves and branches as gravity lures it back to the earth. The web of plant life traps the humidity that, in turn, does its best to destroy everything it touches. Mold forms almost immediately on anything damp. Paper crumbles apart. Items kept inside can become wet purely through exposure to the air and there's always a slightly funny smell somewhere. Clothes left unattended for a day or two start to stink and little green or black spots appear on unmaintained surfaces. I'm having a hard time keeping condensation out of my camera.

At night when we cut the generator and the electric light fades away it becomes so dark that you can't see your palm if you touch it to your face. The jungle growth is so thick you can't see fifteen feet ahead of you in broad daylight.

The girls in the kitchen tell me I'm getting fat, but I warned them about that when they offered free food. I quit taking my vitamins way back in Oaxaca when my little plastic bag full of pills popped a hole and some rainwater worked its way in to make a mess of them all. When the Malaria pills ran out shortly after I didn't bother refilling those, either, and I've given up on insect repellant. I'm happy to report, however, that I'm in good health save for the two toenails I lost on the Mirador trek and a persistent foot pain that I believe I can attribute to bunions. I've constructed arch support for my sandals with pieces of scrap car seat material, foam, and duct tape. They seem to help some. It's hard to believe almost six months have passed and I'm still not even halfway through Guatemala. Tierra del Fuego is still a long way away.

Well, I can't say I'm not enjoying myself or learning a whole lot of new things. Dennis is a wizard at woodworking and as soon as I finish the paintings I'm working on I plan to take some lessons from him. We have a whole swamp full of half rotten, easily salvageable wood to experiment with.

Come on out and visit if you feel wild (call... there's no computer) or I'll be in touch again in the near future. All the best to everyone and I hope the new year is shaping up agreeably for you!

Much love, Dave.

// divided by necessity and desire // tongues flip-flop from different points of the globe // not had much luck // pulse of the jungle // the sky growled, groaned, roared and sent down sheets upon sheets of thick, watery wetness // tree fell last night // skinny dipping in the river // feel like I'm passing through an IMAX film // cut a fishing net with the propeller // an ideal place to come to terms with yourself // haven't had a day off in almost three months // Halloween mascot // disconnection with the power and beauty of life // little fireball // bewitching eyes // old world customs // sliced my toes up pretty deeply // I love this river // friction brewing // birds start their beautiful songs a little too early for me // "whatever is, is right" // have a hard time engaging or being engaged in conversation // vice on my brain // enveloped in a screen of smoke // farmers are burning their fields // adds a somewhat haunting, mysterious air // sitting on the dock of the bay... once again //

From: **Paco Paco** (pacogardenrecords@hotmail.com)
Sent: Thu 5/24/07 11:18 AM
To: **All Friends** (amigos@everywhere.com)
Subject: **Update from the River.**

Friends and Family, Brother and Sisters...

Writing to you again from the Hotel Finca
Tatin, nearing the end of my fifth month of service and
leisure here. Life on the river remains generally slow,
quiet and peaceful, however the days do flash by like
lightning -- illuminating happy children splashing at the
riverbanks in liberating, sun-soaked games of the
season. So subtle is the arrival of summer in regards to
the weather that the more notable changes are those
tangible such as the emergence of seasonal fruit or
certain flowers in bloom. The rains have receded and we
seldom receive, now, more than a spit or two a week. In
the absence of water the oppressive finger of humidity
has been lifted somewhat but in its place festers a
forceful heat that lends its hand to the generation of the
ill-favored vampire flies ("tábanos") who challenge, in
numbers and obscenity, the slightest attempt at
concentration or relaxation. The irksome devils buzz
and bite to no end! It's only a matter of seconds
between the eradication of one and the onset of
another... and they're terribly resilient. So much so, that
if you don't bother to squash and crush them properly,
they're bound to shake off the swat and fly away, sure
to bite you again later. Try as I might, I can find but
little sympathy for these assholes. I take great pleasure
in watching the ants systematically disassemble and

carry off their body parts, like little mechanics salvaging useful scraps from a wrecking yard. I laugh vengefully as they march past me with a wing, a leg, a head, or a crumpled torso. Bloodsuckers! They deserve it.

As for the other animals, I continue to be amazed daily by the quantity and diversity of tropical life that exposes itself here and there as creatures creeping, crawling, gliding, flying, hiding, waiting, and watching all throughout the jungle. My favorite of these is an insect I've never seen, but through some manner of bodily manipulation secretes a sound something similar to that of a whistler bottle rocket that accelerates to peak at the high whine of a table saw and then fizzles out like the dusty last gasp of a witch's laugh or the stubborn creaky hinge of a door. Also among them are the fire fly lightning bugs who set out around dusk to dance through the trees like fairies at a forest ball; big black grasshoppers, trimmed in yellow stripe like the uniformed members of a sports team; deceptive stick bugs; airborne and accident-prone drunk beetles; foot-sized toads who rattle in the night; sleek, playful river otters; black velvet butterflies; and birds of all songs including those who whistle that classic grandfathers' tune.

I loose track of the passing days but every so often stop and reflect on how easy it is to become comfortable here. When you receive friendly waves from everyone on the river, stop for a cold drink or two with friends in town, get to know the shopkeepers by name you begin to feel a part of the community. I've not worn my shoes but twice since I've been here and rarely bother to put on much more than a swimsuit. Anything more is quite unnecessary since I spend a good portion of my time either in the river or a hammock.

Every so often I feel creative and I've been dangerously seduced by nature's sweet fingerprint impressed upon the grains, textures and colors of the tropical hardwoods. Dennis has entrusted me in the use of his carving chisels and with these sharp metal teeth I try and charm the wood out of its fibers and allow them to be cut and reshaped as to realize the form of my "art," though it rarely does what I want. After completing a couple of carvings I've set my sights to learn some of the more technical angles of woodworking, such as box making, which I eventually hope to incorporate with carving when I can make better sense of the two. In observation of the way in which interests and appreciations change with the time I find myself in a new relationship with wood and its source... intriguing materials I've not paid too much attention to in the past.

In a moment of fleeting ambition I thought to employ an opportunity and pick up what I could from the myriad of languages that pass through the hotel. But, already committing a small slice of my day to study Spanish, I soon found myself light-headed with French phrases, Q'eqchi' jokes, and Hebrew meal blessings running all around my brain and I've since decided to limit my information intake, for the time being, to concentrate on Spanish, history, wood, and relaxation.

These little pastimes are squeezed into the slow seconds between normal hotel operations and, even then, I can never fully devote myself to any one project at a time as I must always keep one ear to the telephone, one eye on the dock, and a hand ready to swat invading bloodsuckers. Progress is slow.

To unwind a little after dark I enjoy venturing out into the river with the wooden canoe. I couldn't recreate with words the sensation of laying back in the boat beneath the star-spangled sky, coasting along crystalline black waters, all wrapped up in the untamed chatter of the night. When the full moon makes its rounds and sprinkles its light softly over the horizon, its twin sister mirrored on the water's surface below, I feel as if I'm flying through space, enveloped in nothingness.

I've also grown fond of occasionally driving the motorboat into town to pick up groceries or clients. The majesty of the canyon, to me, still retains its luster and I can't help but smile every time I pass through it. Past the watchful eyes of herons perched like sentinels at the river's edge... beneath the shadows of giant pelicans circling overhead, bearing a strong resemblance to the long gone pterodactyl, eyeing the river for unsuspecting fish at which they silently cannonball themselves, exploding into the water and swallowing whole and alive the unfortunate laggard. The winds pick up as we ride out into the bay pushing up small swells against which the boat pushes back, sending up spray, dipping and rolling as we cut through waves and bounce over the choppy waters.

I imagine the life of sailors far out in the open sea fighting to keep afloat through the furious hiss and crash of a pounding storm. I snap out of the daydream briefly to apply all senses to docking the boat, the art of which I'm still working to perfect. But the wind soon calls out to me from the sea, whispering tiny reminders of my own little journey and that I should soon be back on the road, sinking south towards my destination.

Much love until next time, Dave.

P.S.- I apologize sincerely for the great delay or complete lack of response to many emails. I get to the computer more often now than before, but in short spurts between all else. I have read and appreciate all mail, but have fallen behind due to my erratic in-town schedule. I promise to keep up if we can start a fresh slate, okay?

// a night of tortuous headache, tossing, turning, and puking // stealing people and/or their body parts // what vanity to assume this crooked human race to be the peak of evolution // don't really want to pack my bag and put on my shoes // beautifully bright double rainbow // 20 minutes the wrong way // full of sweet smells // vegan Japanese dinner // 11th ruin site this trip. They start to look the same // ate peanuts and cookies in the graveyard // crested in green with cobblestone streets // feel as if I'm in high school again // border patrol officers at the check point between Guatemala and Honduras eating ice cream cones from the ice cream truck // black romantic // hell ride bus // clutch air line broke // the devilish eyes // I wanted to die // feel it burning inside // drank red wine on the balcony // impossible to go anywhere in Guatemala without making friends // drop off cliffs, dazzling views // I think I smell bad, but I can't tell anymore // passed the whole day waiting // her body was discovered half eaten by animals and maggots // laugh and pull the rug out from under me // they're burning incense in the cemetery and the birds are singing // made friends with the immigration officials // peek through a dirty, broken window // didn't feel like the bus hassle and came to the beach instead // hungry, dirty, and tired as hell // I think I made a new record for myself at 8 buses in one day // shower smells like the elephant cage at the zoo // lost $40 at the border // really beginning to look the same // sink my teeth into her throat // the thought of 10 more hours on the bus made me want to puke // museum nothing more than photocopies taped to poster board // pretty, little waterfall // terrible attraction to tragedy //

dinner at a little under a dollar // feel lazy // reminded me of Cabrini Green // surrounded by bats // there's a blackout in the city tonight and the bugs are killing me //

From: **Paco Paco** (pacogardenrecords@hotmail.com)
Sent: Sat 7/28/07 9:38 PM
To: **All Friends** (amigos@everywhere.com)
Subject: **Back in the Saddle Again.**

Friends and Family, Brothers and Sisters...

After a stay of nearly six months at the Hotel Finca Tatin I found myself one morning in mid-June floating down the river with my bags packed back in the direction of the highway and the trip I had put on hold for what, at the time, had seemed so long but now, in motion again, doesn't seem but a couple of weeks. Once on the road I stopped first at the small town and Mayan ruins of Quiriguá and then at the world famous ruins of Copán (Honduras). These two sites feature gracefully detailed stone block stelae in the forms of ancient rulers or animal gods. The statues stare at you from behind faces both proud and bold. Through vacant eyes and set jaws, but there are a few whose gaze is a touch more human, who wear a somber, sage expression of humility. The carvings are impressive and imaginative and hint a little as to where George Lucas got some of his Star Wars ideas.

I passed then through Guatemala City and was graced for many days by the warm, untiring hospitality of a friend's family there. Not wanting to wear out my welcome I said goodbye and made my way by bus up into the Guatemalan highlands. The buses out this way are something else. From just about anywhere in town you can catch one of these hot rods painted up like circus transportation or amusement park rides with colored/flashing strobe lights all over and destination nameplates that read like rainbow Ouija boards. When the bus you want passes you flag him down, grab hold of a chrome plated handle, swing yourself on board and, if you're lucky, take a seat or balance yourself on the edge of one. If not, hang on to something quick as the nihilistic bus driver, crazed with adrenaline, slams the beast into gear, pins the gas pedal to the floor and, jolted and with a crunch of metal, you erupt forward like a bat out of hell in this Easter Egg rocket. In and out of doors and windows and up and over the moving bus like a monkey climbs the ticket man to help load, tie, unload and untie packages and bags or squish more people in, take their money, and issue their tickets. The bus flies like a wild dragon, growling and grunting, spitting fire and smoke as it claws its way up the mountainside, whipping its long body through blind curves against oncoming traffic as it rips past other trucks or buses, roaring and rumbling, stopping periodically and only very briefly to cough up a few passengers or swallow others anew before it grinds its round rubber claws into the earth, snorts, sputters, and shoots off again in a puff of smoke towards the sky.

I arrived in Quetzaltenango pleased by the pleasant, fresh climate, colonial architecture, and a lot less garbage and exhaust than exist back in the capitol. Quetzaltenango ("Xela"), the second largest city, is home to many foreigners and is a major tourist stop and, thanks to this, I was able to find plenty of tasty, moderately priced vegetarian food. Surrounded by mountains and filled with friendly people it really is a nice town.

Here in Central America volcanoes are... I wouldn't say quite as common as Starbucks Coffee in the States... but not far off. It seems that every third or fourth hill is a cone with a crater. The only one I've climbed so far, though, was the Santa Maria outside of Xela. The city bus took me out to the start of the trail and from there I hiked about an hour or so to the base of the volcano. Once on the mountain, whoever originally cut the trail didn't bother with many switchbacks or "make it easy to hike" baloney and the path leads more or less straight up to the top. At some points I might as well have been climbing a ladder. Two more tough hours later I arrived at the peak to find myself all wrapped up in a cloud with nothing to see but pure white in every direction. A real shame because the Santa Maria sits overlooking a smaller live volcano named "Santiaguito" and I've heard the views of both that and the landscape beyond are spectacular. Well, on this particular day I didn't see a damned thing. I took a seat on a rock and not more than two minutes passed when I heard a deep rolling rumble which I first mistook to be one of the minor daily eruptions from Santiaguito, but as I couldn't see where, at all, the other volcano lay I wasn't quite sure. The thundering continued, now from all around, and I soon realized I was standing in the middle of a storm cloud. Still tired from the trek to the top I wanted to rest and wait out the storm -- hopefully sneak a peek at the "view" -- but the thought of getting licked by a bolt of lightning up on a bald mountaintop all by my lonesome altered my thinking and I decided to try for a retreat back towards town before the rain came. I was too late, of course. The minute I set foot on the trail the clouds burst and sent forth sheets of water accompanied by pelting dime and nickel-sized hail. Planning like a boy scout I had brought with me my Trusty Tarp, through the center of which I'd cut a little hole for my little head and I can now use it as a plastic poncho on the rainy days. In the true spirit of procrastination I still haven't attached a hood, but luckily the hood of my sweatshirt absorbed a good deal of water as well as the sting of the hail and Trusty Tarp kept relatively dry the upper two thirds of my body. Meanwhile, down around my shoes, however, the dirt path, collecting an incredible amount of water and hail, had churned itself into a wild, miniature, muddy river that worked wonders at taking my feet out from under me. I slid and twisted and tumbled toward the base of the mountain at an alarming rate but still managed to maintain the outward appearance of "carrying myself upright" even if the appearance may have been that of someone slightly intoxicated. All around me raged the storm. The crash and flash of lightning and thunder squeezed tightly together into the same split second -- too real, too close for comfort. At every blast the earth shook as if slapped by the angry god who, huffing and puffing, burned at my heels, chasing me back down to civilization. For a good forty-five minutes I was assaulted by hail and the rain didn't tire out until, another forty-five minutes later, I'd nearly reached the trailhead. When it did and I stopped to breathe and shake myself out a bit (check for missing limbs and

60

electrical burns) I turned to look once again at the volcano and wasn't surprised to see the peak, perfectly clear, shimmering against a calm, blue sky. Not a cloud within reach.

From Quetzaltenango I climbed higher up into the mountains to the town of Todos Santos Cuchumatán, which reclines sleepily in a misty valley just barely bowing its head below the swimming, dancing clouds swirling at speeds throughout the sky above. From these giants every so often a smaller member wrestles itself clear to drift mindlessly, creeping with its fingers over the hills, occasionally arrested, snagged on the trees like cotton candy stuck on Velcro. The inhabitants of Todos Santos are proud of their heritage and preserve an old tradition in their clothing. All the men wear red and white-striped pants, white and dark-striped jackets with colorfully knitted collars, and small sombreros haloed each by a little blue belt. The women wear dark tops with colorfully woven design, black with blue-striped long skirts, and braid their hair. When seen all together in the street they look like a sports team or band of clowns en route to an event.

I also made a short visit to the town of Panajachel on the Lake of Atitlán with its three volcanoes, Chihicastenango and the artisans' market, Antigua, and Amatitlán.

On the way out of Guatemala the feelings of nostalgia and sadness consumed me. Like a thread from my heart still wound around something I had left behind, tugging and unraveling itself more and more with every mile. Like that feeling of breaking up with a good girlfriend. That uncertain but hopeful feeling of knowing you're walking away from something good but there might be something better yet ahead.

With these thoughts I crossed the border into El Salvador, stopped in the capitol of San Salvador for a few days, and then out towards the beautiful black sand beaches of the Pacific Coast.

At Zunzal I watched the surfers dance weightlessly over the waves until the sun burned itself out and sank, like a hulled ship, beneath the horizon. The last splash in its struggle for life caught by the clouds and spread through the sky like the smoke and flame of a late autumn's bonfire.

On to Nicaragua. I rolled into León on the 19th of July, the day now celebrated as the Anniversary of the Revolution in remembrance of that date in 1979 when the FSLN first took control of Managua. León, however, was the first city taken during the struggle and, for this, is dubbed the "Capitol of the Revolution." As I arrived the outskirts of town were flooded with buses, marchers, banners, and the red and black flag of the FSLN (National Sandonista Liberation Front). The colonial center of town was quiet in comparison with hardly anyone in the streets and almost all doors closed. I had a little trouble finding a room and a meal.

I passed through the many murals of Estelí, through the slums, flies, and beggars of Managua, and write to you now from Granada on the banks of Lake Nicaragua. From here I will pass further south along the lake and then over to the Island of Ometepe and visit a couple of organic farms there.

Hope all is well with you wherever you are and that the summer is passing pleasantly.

Until next time...

Love, Dave.

// morning in Poets' Park // worse than the flies // waiting for the bus to monkey island // too much time to think // walked back to the hotel barefoot and bare-chested // missed the bus twice // dead sick of being a tourist // the Spanarchists lied to me // nature living outside of human stress and constraint // surfers, hot girls in bikinis // the electricity comes and goes // walked in circles under the burning sun // this is my kind of place // found some AC/DC songs on the computer // a year since I left // middle of a wind tunnel // nothing to do, nowhere to go // now they lost their wings and disappeared // the streets flood, the market floods, the roof leaks // found a turtle skull // slept most of the night on the beach // disgusting, weird, comfortable, bright, sterile // got hit in the leg by a falling rock // live in a corrugated tin shack with a failing scrap wood floor // scared them off with my ill rhythm and savage sweat // found a Lebanese snack shack at the border // through the ruins of the old Panama that were destroyed by old Captain Henry Morgan // it's not the destination, it's the travel in-between //

From: **Paco Paco** (pacogardenrecords@hotmail.com)
Sent: Thu 9/20/07 6:10 PM
To: **All Friends** (amigos@everywhere.com)
Subject: **Volcanoes of Nicaragua to the Panama Canal.**

Friends and Family, Brothers and Sisters...

Hurricane Felix has passed and the Atlantic Coast of Nicaragua licks its wounds and begins to sew itself back together. I've left León where I had taken up residence for a month while working as a volunteer tour guide for an organization called "Quetzaltrekkers" that raises money to help homeless and abused children in Nicaragua (and Guatemala) by offering guided trips to some of the active volcanoes in the area. The money gained from the hikes is donated to support programs run by "Las Tias" group to get young children out of the work force and into schools, provide shelter for the homeless, and give sanctuary as well as psychological support to physically or sexually abused and neglected children.

My time, however, was not spent with the children but up in the hills hacking through trails and hauling camping gear up to the summits of the smoldering giants that make up the Maribios volcanic range stretching from Lake Managua northwest towards the Honduran border. Like a fingerprint each volcano is distinctly unique and after hours of dragging your body and bag uphill against the sun, sweat, bugs, and mud each presents an unforgettable and rewarding view of the Nicaraguan landscape. Strolling through the craters shrouded in sulfur smoke feels like walking on an alien planet. Dizzy from the gases, hissing as they escape air vents in the crust, you slide and stumble across warm, rust colored mud and burned yellow soil followed by a harem of oddly colored insects. Outside, the craters are crowned in loose lava rock and black sand (inclined, at times, to a nearly 45 degree angle where a false step or mighty strong wind could send you tumbling from the mountain) that we traverse to reach and return from the peak. Those energetic and daring like to run down the sandy slope skidding three or four feet with each step or just sliding all the way down as if on invisible skis. Another company in town promotes "volcano boarding" in which they send folks downhill on sleds and claim to have reached speeds of 60 MPH. Some volcanoes are classic in shape like pimples raised by an adolescent earth purging its pores and other are just gaping holes left in rolling hills -- a series of odd exits piled up on top of one another like the crust of a charred pizza somebody put their fingers through. Watching the crisp sunrise over Volcán Telica or waiting from the side of Momotombo to watch the late afternoon fireball fall between volcanoes Asososca and San Cristóbal painted for me sweet and rich images I won't soon forget.

Quetzaltrekkers is run strictly by volunteers, the information and responsibilities passed down to new hands with no one technically "in charge." This means that when all are on the ball the system works, but all days can't be perfect and the organization could be a bit more organized. When not hiking I got to get artsy designing magazine ads, promotional flyers, postcards, etc. I put to use some of my spare time by drawing up and printing a touristy t-shirt design to sell and help me get along a little in my travels. It didn't help much. T-shirts are costly to make and can't be sold for much here, but it was fun to pass the time.

León is one of Nicaragua's few centers of arts and learning and is more culturally progressive and open than many other parts of the country. It boasts a healthy nightlife and much live music. The streets are often filled with university students jogging between classes or people just out jogging for exercise. There is, as there is anywhere, an uncomfortable contrast between those educated and aware and those held down by ignorance and in-exposure. As I sat in the central plaza selling my t-shirts I watched some so quick to toss their trash in the street like a hot potato and others who would cross the entire plaza to put it in the trash can. Boys yelling crude and macho catcalls at passing girls and others buying ice cream and opening the doors for their girlfriends. The times are changing and it's interesting, yet sometimes frustrating, to see the process in motion.

In all, the majority of the people in León and Nicaragua are exceedingly friendly, helpful, and generous. León, being near the Pacific Coast, caught only the tail end of the hurricanes that whipped at us some heavy, heavy rains and lively thunderstorms. The rainy season is passing but the weather was still unbearably hot and humid and I'm at a loss as to understand how anyone unaccustomed to the climate could make a life there.

While in the country I also spent some lazy days at an organic farm nestled between the twin volcanoes of the island Ometepe on the impressively large puddle of water they call Lake Nicaragua (8624 sq. km supplied by 45 rivers). I felt like an explorer in a King Kong movie arriving by ferry from the mainland at the base of Volcán Concepción, but the island is actually much more populated and developed than I had imagined. On the south end, though, you can still lose yourself in the tropical forest under the watchful eyes of howler monkeys crawling through the trees above.

After a few dips in the sea at the beaches of Las Peñitas, San Juan del Sur, and Maderas I was off to Costa Rica, just passing through as the price of life there is a little more than my humble budget will allow and the country doesn't offer much that I haven't seen in other parts of Central America. I did spend a couple days in San José and can say that Costa Rica is leaps and bounds ahead of northern Central America. It's much more developed, far less dirty, and the people seem to be somewhat freer from constrictive traditions.

I write to you now from Panama City, lost in the meandering streets as they squish themselves into an unending grid, crammed with traffic and shadowed by towers of concrete, glass and steel poking and slicing at the sky like aggravated sound waves or a bed of nails. A shiny modern maze fed by the rat race of human

70

society. Panama City reminds me in ways of a western Singapore. A crossroads and melting pot of the races and religions who, in the past, came to build the Canal and those who come now to do business in the city that it created. The economy here must really be booming, although they tell me not as many boats pass through as before. The city is growing at an astonishing rate and it's hard to tell which buildings are complete and which are in the works what for the amount of cranes and raw materials lying around. The sidewalks are overrun with promotion for one thousand and one new construction projects to squeeze into the cracks between existing high-rises and corroding slums.

I made a visit today in the rain to the Panama Canal to watch some Panamax freight barges squeeze though the nearly one hundred year-old locks towards the Pacific. It's interesting to watch on TV, but it's really impressive to see up close. The size of the barges themselves is mind blowing and to think that any power other than Yoda's Force or Mother Nature could manipulate and move them is... well, you'd have to see it up close.

Tomorrow I'm off to the Caribbean Coast to see about catching a sailboat over to Cartagena, Colombia. I hope this little note finds you all well and happy. See you around...

Love, Dave.

// I can't move without sweating. I sweat without moving // litter, litter, litter, hustlers, beggars, idiots // the moon shakes, she shines, she's like a hole in the sky to the wild world outside // time for siesta // sat in the shade of the tall palms in the plaza // sucked into the television // bed is as hard as a rock // I think I walked 6000 miles today // these cops aren't complete meatheads // talked myself stupid last night about politics and socialism // walking party hunter // will the rain ever stop? // offered me a job carving wood // bought cookies and bananas and watched a movie on TV // told them I couldn't pay more than 9 and they let me in for 6 // the old men with their hats standing around in the park // Sepultura played a free concert last night under the metro track // sick of eating rice and beans // drank a bottle of aguardiente // big fat veggie burger // sweet flower fragrance and bird song in the air // warm, colorful sunset // having withdrawals from Medellín // rearranging everything in my stomach // the only girls that wanted to talk to me were the drag queens on the corner // my flip-flops broke and I dropped my sweet bread in the gutter // Sunday morning market // two semi trucks smashed into each other and one fell off the bridge //

From: **Paco Paco** (pacogardenrecords@hotmail.com)
Sent: Wed 11/07/07 4:21 PM
To: **All Friends** (amigos@everywhere.com)
Subject: **Colombia / Notes from the Equator.**

Friends and Family, Brothers and Sisters…

My hopes for traveling by sailboat from Colón to Cartagena were squashed when I arrived at the Caribbean Coast to find that a boat had just left two days before and there might not be another for the next week, two weeks, or even another month. So I sat at the municipal dock in Colón for three days to see if anything was moving but the only remote possibility was a cargo ship heading to some island off the Colombian coast at some unspecified date whose captain was mysteriously never around to talk to. So I waited but as the crumbling, forsaken town of Colón has deteriorated into a wasted ghetto where foreigners are regularly robbed at gunpoint in broad daylight and the police ride around two to the back of beat up dirt bikes in full body armor, one driving, the other caressing a twelve-gauge shotgun as they speed through the streets keeping watch over the poor village, I felt that three days was enough. There are still no overland roads to cross the Darien Gap so, more or less out of options, I caved-in and, with my tail between my legs, limped back to Panama City and bought a plane ticket.

So I missed the San Blas Islands and exquisite Caribbean waters but arrived in Cartagena happy and ready to take on South America. Though Colombia's internal battles have diminished in recent years the country still struggles to throw off a bad reputation of violence, narco-terrorism, and civil war but I found it to be one of the most beautiful countries I've ever stepped foot in. From its cherished colonial architecture, its rich, colorful, and majestic landscapes, sleepy haciendas, delightfully friendly people, world renowned, painfully gorgeous women, coffee plantations, indigenous villages, and abundant fauna and flora it's impossible to evade enchantment. I traveled north from the old walled city of Cartagena, once the passageway to South America protected by its canons and forts, up to Santa Marta and the famous beaches around the Tayrona National Park, tucked into bays and coves along the northern shore. There I met up with my buddy Carlos from the Finca Tatin and we spent about a week floating around the plazas and outdoor cafés of tiny mountain towns in the coffee sector like San Gil, Barichara, and Villa de Leyva where the air is fresh, the weather perfect, and the scenery outstanding. If you could erase the modern people and their cars you would swear to be lost in the past, wandering among uniformly whitewashed buildings and aging cobblestone streets. We passed many a tranquil hour watching the world go by in the company of fresh juice and a pleasant breeze. Yes, yes I know. Life is hard, but we do what we can. It's most difficult when that deadly sweet, intoxicating, captivating, and unmistakable aroma drifts from the bakery doors out into the streets. When it sinks its hooks into your olfactory registration and you're obliged, like a drooling bloodhound, to put your nose to the scent until you've tracked down a little shop full of way too

76

much sugary stuff than can be good for anyone but, before you know it, you're walking out with one of everything.

I had planned to stop by Lake Guatavita from where stems the legend of "El Dorado" on my way south, however visitors are apparently only allowed on weekends and even then not without a special government-issued permission form. As I was passing through on a Tuesday I just let the legend lie.

A return to chaos in the big city when I arrived in Bogotá and had to shift gears to keep up with the thousands of metropolitan men and women streaming through the crowded streets in the dance of urban distraction. I took a cheap room in the historic Candelaria district and spent the days and nights conversing with college students, admiring hilltop views of the city, exploring back alley rock and reggae bars, and kicking around at weekend flea markets and free concerts. Bogotá is home to nearly uncountable parks, universities, bookshops, theatres, and is famous for its nightlife and music scene. Thanks to the Hare Krishnas I was able to find vegetarian restaurants there and in every other big city in Colombia.

From Bogotá I stopped in Manizales and Pereira on the way to Medellín where I fell in love with the "most progressive" city, maybe because it reminds me somewhat of Denver blessed with the weather of L.A. I got mighty comfortable at the hotel there and loved to sit on the balcony with new friends and watch the stop and go traffic of the cars and how the motorcycles flowed through and around them like little drops of water running down a wall. Medellín boasts Colombia's only metro train, which is also connected to a gondola system that transports commuters up a hillside in one of the poorer districts. For the price of a standard metro ticket you can ride all around town and up the hillside to take advantage of the wonderful views of the city day or night.

With some effort I eventually summoned up the will power to jump on a bus out of Medellín but beforehand, around Halloween, I spent a wild night up in the mountains behind the city on a "soul searching vision quest" with a medicine man from the Amazon and a cup of the Amazonian medicine "yagé" (a.k.a. "Ayahuasca"). The so-called medicine is made from a combination of tropical vines whose toxic juices, when ingested, send you into a trance as you travel through your inner self to confront hidden fears or weaknesses and come to terms with your dark sides and demons. The latter are believed by the jungle tribes to be expelled in the form of vomit and diarrhea, which plague the remainder of your psychedelic ride, unrelenting, until way into the next day. Purifying chants and traditional rituals are performed before, as needed during, and after your voyage. A fire is kept burning at your feet to guide you through the night. Smoke from incense and sacred herbs mixes with that of the fire and they dance away together into the darkness. The full moon illuminates in a timid blue haze the forest all around and the pine needle bedding in the shaman's shack is soft and smells fresh. When the early morning sun breaks and you reacquaint yourself with the physical world the shaman again blesses and cleanses you and you can chat with him about your trip.

So, still feeling rotten in the stomach, I caught a bus down to Cali for a few days, Colombia's salsa music capitol, and then up winding mountain roads to the indigenous village of Silvia. The guerrilla threat there is still very strong and fully armed and equipped green-beret soldiers patrol the streets rain or shine with monster Rottweilers and occasional military helicopters making rounds overhead. The village, however, parted by a frothing river, is precious -- the air laced with the scent of coffee and mint, and the locals in their traditional fashion are cute and hospitable. It had been raining a lot and whenever it did stop it didn't stop for long. I arrived in Popayán wet and muddy. The historic center of Popayán has retained and repaired what it could from various earthquake shakes and holds rigidly to maintaining the colonial white walls giving a bright nucleus to the urban sprawl that has grown out beyond. The city lies in a valley surrounded by pine and bamboo forests and a grass-like green carpet that falls in wrinkles and ripples over the ridges and folds of mountainsides down into canyons cut by raging rivers, swallowed by the empty mists below.

I've seen a whole lot of churches on this trip but nothing like the Salt Cathedral in the salt mines of Zipaquirá. Originally for the use of the miners, this wonder has been carved deep below the surface into pure salt deposits -- a tunnel uniting various others that represents the stations-of-the-cross, eventually emptying into a huge subterranean church adorned sparsely with salt, granite, or marble statues and neon lights. The complex constitutes a labyrinth of rambling stairs and passageways, all carved directly into the rock salt as it lay, like an amusement park of minimalist religious art for the new age.

Another impressive church was the Sanctuary at Las Lajas near Ipiales where appeared to a mother and daughter, traveling along the canyon of the Guáitara River around 1750, a painting of the Virgin Mary on a rock believed to be a miracle manifestation of the virgin herself. It is a customary belief that she helps those who pass and many make pilgrimages there or leave name plaques to score points with her. The community has erected three successive temples on top of each other at the site and the final is a gothic basilica that stretches, with the help of a bridge, from one canyon wall across the river to the other. Its beauty is accentuated by a tall, tumbling waterfall nearby.

I write to you now from Quito in the cool Andes of Ecuador sitting on the belt of the equator. Ecuador seems to have a lot to offer but I'll leave that to the next chapter.

Until then...

Love, Dave.

// amazing how moody I can be // ate fruit on a bench in the warm sun // couldn't find spit for veggie food // just doesn't understand. I don't know if I do, either // I'm bored, and annoyed by everything, and scared to commit to anything // insisted on buying me cookies and sweets // countless hours of high school marching bands // educate the locals in a way that embraces their traditional heritage // dirty, polluted, ignorant // proceeded to drink about 6000 Black Russians // wished like hell that I was dead // felt a little earthquake // trying to practice the Buddhists' law of non-desire to attain happiness // harder and harder to choke down rice and beans // stomach's all screwed up // under a complete double rainbow // baby cried all night // locals vs. tourists and tourist vs. tourist // chickens and roosters are the stupidest, most annoying birds // suppose I should fix my shoes // if aliens came to the planet and asked, "What is life?" I would take them to the market // education is the key... damn sure of it // in better spirits today // her soul stuck right on me // the bed is as hard as packed sand, but it's even // "Daddy, let's go do it... $3" // restaurant that gives you free weed with your meals // away from the pool and pretty girls // steal a peddle boat // sick of thinking about money // held the forgotten feeling of utter desolation // drank Cuba Libres and danced until way after the sun had come up // walked 3 or 4 hours and sang songs // these smell like death // always something, always nothing // fuck 'em, I ate carrots // found some yucca and fried plátano // I think I've walked a total of 18 or 19 hours in the past three days // talked with a small circle of old wrinkly guys // old junker and my knees were squashed into the seat in front of me // ugly, wasted town // my toenail is surely dead // terrible lightning and thunder // bad news at the border // I haven't been in one place for more than three days since... //

From: **Paco Paco** (pacogardenrecords@hotmail.com)
Sent: Fri 12/21/07 2:58 AM
To: **All Friends** (amigos@everywhere.com)
Subject: **The Road to Machu Picchu.**

Friends and Family, Brothers and Sisters...

Sitting on the edge of a tiny creek watching the trash float by. A plastic bag passes with a crisp, crinkled gasp and then an old two-liter bottle of something that echoes like an artificial drum as it bounces off the rocks and tumbles downstream followed by a tin can rolling and clattering along like a stout, stubborn army sergeant. Together they sing an outcast song as the river carries them away. I've seen more trash here in Peru than in most of Colombia or Ecuador. Some stretches of the highway in the northern desert cut through towns so littered with plastic refuse that the inhabitants literally walk little paths worn between endless piles of garbage. This isn't seen at the well-known sites. The "gringo trail" is kept pretty clean, but not without cost. Peru is relatively cheap to travel but the price gorging at the tourist sites is unbelievable. Up to 9 or 10 times market value, if not more. This may be good for their economy but not for a lone traveler of humble budget such as myself.

I last left you in Quito, Ecuador's capitol city, whose throbbing growth is confined to a narrow valley in the North Andes. It rolls out in either direction like a snake that has consumed the old colonial center along with its famously adorned churches and vigorous theatre productions, the new center of commerce and entertainment districts and numerous parks and museums. It was raining a lot in Quito so I hopped down the road and rented a bicycle to visit the hot springs and waterfalls around the pleasant tourist town of Baños, situated near the Tungurahua volcano. I passed Ambatos and Cuenca, Riobamba and the well-known market of Otavalo up north. I love the Latin American markets. Walking into one can be a shock to the system at first. Something like a Las Vegas casino with its wild carpets, the rattling "ching ching" of the bell machines, mirrors, lights, and flying cards. The market also immediately assaults the senses from all sides. A hurricane of hustlers guarantee you "special prices" on a myriad of goods -- "anything you're looking for." A rainbow of fruits and vegetables stacked artfully from the floor up; the rich, confusing scent of hundreds of herbs and spices mingles with that of dead fish; all the flavors of fresh juice imaginable; watch and shoe repairmen; children playing among the butchered remains of animal carcasses; colorful cloth and bags overflowing with seed and grain; enticing sweet breads and candies; out front taxi drivers competing for fares and vendors promoting their wares over loudspeakers rigged to the tops of their bicycle carts; dueling sound systems blaring opposing tunes; a sidewalk of open sores hungry and waiting to swallow whole the foot or leg of anyone unaware; ice cream; shoe shines; medicines both natural and pharmaceutical; dress clothes; dinky plastic toys; and more... What may have been overwhelming at first soon becomes comfortable and convenient.

I arrived in the teeny tiny town of Vilcabamba towards the south with a terrible intestinal infection and was laid out for a few days on antibiotics, painkillers, and sleeping pills. When I was able to eat again I made my way into Peru.

Almost the entire west coast of Peru is comprised of vast, barren desert lashed by sandstorms that play at building and reshaping sand dunes in the forms of croissants or slug-like serpents, only occasionally breached by mountains of true rock. The north is littered with archaeological sites and the ruined remains of grand adobe pyramids left by pre-Hispanic civilizations in the areas around Chiclayo and Trujillo (now they look like piles of mud drenched in acid).

From the oasis town of Huacachina, near Ica, I took a dune buggy tour out into this surreal world of windswept hills of yellow sand under the big blue sky that stretches endlessly, like the sea, into the horizon. We brought with us some home-fashioned "sandboards" to shoot ourselves recklessly down the steep slopes, where our driver would meet us at the bottom and haul us in the car jumping, skipping, and sliding up to the crest of the next great hill. I have still to shake all the sand from my hair, ears, toenails, clothes, etc.

Further south I stopped in Nazca to take a short Cessna flight over the mysterious "Nazca Lines" laid out for miles in the hard crust of the desert plain in what is believed to be one of: a) a sort of calendar system, b) a guide to underground water sources, c) a series of ritualistic walking trails, or d) drawings meant to pay homage to the gods. The main attraction to the lines are gigantic animal forms only truly visible from the sky accompanied by trapezoids, unerring straight lines between the hills, and confusing spirals -- all of which have led some folks to believe that the lines are some sort of alien landing strips or extra terrestrial communications. The ancient pre-Inca peoples, who are thought to have left these lines, buried their dead in shallow underground tombs at a site now about 20 km outside the town of Nazca. The bodies were mummified and adorned with jewelry and pottery for a head start in the next life which later drew the attention of tomb raiders who dug up the mummies, ripped apart their burial wraps to get at the goods inside, and scattered the worthless bones and remains about the rocky flatlands where they were later discovered by scientists studying the lines. The better-preserved mummies are displayed in their open-air tombs, some with dreadlocks up to two meters long, preserved still by the dry, arid climate. The grounds of the cemetery lie speckled even now with a quantity of sun-bleached human bones. I certainly wanted to take a few souvenirs, but thought it disrespectful as well as it would put me at a disadvantage with customs officials.

I took a night bus from Nazca up to the attractive and lively colonial town of Cusco. From there I started off on a back roads journey to Machu Picchu by way of the towns and ruins of Pisac and Ollantaytambo, through the sacred valley of the Incas where the early morning sun shines its first lazy rays over the hilltops, flooding the farmers' fields with the light of the new day. The alternating crops and cuts fill the valley, like water balancing itself, to create a patchwork design that compliments the patterns of the ceramic tiled roofs of the pueblos and weaves an image not unlike a woman's dress in a Klimt painting. Low riding clouds wrap themselves without concern around radiant green hills, fingering the pale grey sky and the obscure jagged peaks that rip through them, overshadowed at times by a white-capped goliath far off in the distance whose new dusting of snow dies slowly in an icy trail of tears running down the cracks of the slope into rivers and streams below. Locals in their candy-colored garments, top hats, and long braids come down from the highlands, frostbite scars on their children's cheeks, to sell handicraft art and food in the town markets until the cyclops blaze of the sun surrenders, smothered by the evening haze, and concedes to shut his eye and share his kingdom with the moon and her crystalline stars until the tired, rocky world spins itself around to face him again at dawn.

With my surroundings as such I set out on foot from the end of the road near Ollantaytambo to walk the remaining 30 km to Machu Picchu by way of the railroad tracks that run along the Urubamba River. It was a pleasant walk, although a little long and the rocks and wooden beams really did a number on my feet. It rained and drizzled most of the time, but I suppose that's better than the hot sun and I passed four or five other ruin sites on the way. I would have liked to take the train, but it's disgustingly overpriced and the old

Inca trail that runs back through the mountains is off limits to anyone who doesn't pay $200-$300 USD for a guided tour. Even walking the tracks is prohibited and I nearly broke my neck a few times scaling cliffs or ducking into forests to avoid guard shacks. I lost my footing once descending from a high field back to the trail line, barely holding myself there with my hands around tree roots and grass and my feet dug into the rocks. I could only watch in horror as the plastic bag of food tied to my back ripped and my oranges, bread, carrots, and nuts tumbled hopelessly off the cliff in front of me. I recovered most of it from the mud and stones below and tried to make what I could of a lunch from that.

I was the first person to arrive at the gates of Machu Picchu the next morning just after sunrise because I was informed wrongly at the base of the mountain that the site would open at 5:00. I started my hike from the bottom at 4:00, but in reality that they don't open until 6:00, so I cursed and grunted about the extra hour I could've slept but when I was allowed in and stood in awe looking over the stones of the cloud city washed in smooth morning sunlight all the sweat, blood, and bruises I endured to get there... all the lost sleep, money spent, achy feet... all faded away. All was worth the trouble and I would do it all over again just to feel anew that calm and secure embrace of an ageless peace, a wisdom that sleeps deep inside every one of us, so often lost or forgotten. But there on the peak of Waynapicchu, gazing from towering heights to the miniature sister city below, breathing in turn the breath of the gods, gently caressed by the sweet breeze of the angels as they pass, so far above the world of chaos and filth festering somewhere far away... life suddenly becomes so simple, so clear. Here where every beat of the heart rumbles through eternity and the pulse of existence is measured by the roar of the distant river and the echoes of the train whistle that bounce and rattle up through the canyon, lost in the rising, drifting mists of a place so magically delightful as to satisfy any young boy's thirst for adventure or little girl's dreams of a lonely princess in a forsaken castle at the edge of time immemorial. The sheer power of the ambience almost swallows the glory of the ruins themselves, but the unfathomably precise masonry of the old city can't be ignored for long. A lost art that would take generations of study to recover stands against time and nature, defiant and beautiful in its testimony to the past. The use of stone both cut and raw, fountains and water channels, meandering stairways, windowed rooms with balconies, and terraced green pastures stirred up in me an envious desire to never leave. Of course I did have to climb down from this pinnacle of dreams (the lunch buffet costs $30!) and get back on my own path towards the south.

Forty-four hours of grueling travel later (a little by foot and the rest between six buses, split nicely by a refreshing dip in the world class hot springs at Santa Teresa) landed me in Arequipa, the second largest city, built widely of white volcanic stone. The third of these six buses was the most entertaining...

I was dead asleep when our bus was stopped around midnight but the nearby sounds of argument and struggle woke me. I didn't much more than crack my eyelids to see a man with a cheap flashlight trying to pry a bag from the hands of another seated in my row. The latter was yelling, "No! Don't take it! I'm just a worker, that's all I have!" The former finally got a hold of the bag and tossed it to another guy in the isle. They then pulled up the seat next to me and drew out a little plastic bag of something and again, the arguing, pushing, pulling, "Give it back!" The rest of the bus sat in petrified silence except where the other guys were rummaging through people's luggage up front and a shiver ran through my heart as I thought, "Jesus! We're being held up! It's a goddamn guerrilla raid!" Now the guy with the flashlight was arguing with two older women nearby and I couldn't for the life of me figure out why, on a second-class bus full of workers and ordinary folk, they hadn't yet bothered me, the only tourist there. I figured they were saving me for last and as I sat with my eyes closed as if still asleep trying not to draw too much attention to myself I slowly pushed my bag back as far as I could beneath the seat thinking, "Damn, the bastards are gonna get me camera... and what's worse all the pictures that are in it." (100% tourist) And as I waited and tried to conjure up some escape from the inevitable, remembering all the stories I'd heard of folks getting shot in the legs for not complying, nothing happened... and still nothing, until finally all went quiet, the bus motor started up, and we were back on the road. I let out a confused sigh of relief and gathered from the emerging conversations and

90

gossip that we had just passed a drug enforcement checkpoint. The aggressive guys with flashlights (and no uniforms!) were task force police, we were on a major drug trafficking route and the passengers seated around me were illegally transporting coca leaves (pre-cocaine, which are actually available at any corner store and used to make tea in any restaurant). In my sleep I had missed the initial announcement and just woke in time to catch the chaos of the search and, as usual in these situations, I, the tourist, was left alone.

Not more than half an hour later, though, the bus was stopped again and I heard a guy outside yell, "Go ahead and get some good sleep! You can't get through on the road ahead!" Apparently due to heavy rains and wind a landslide had buried a small section of the highway about twenty or thirty cars ahead of us. There was no alternate southbound route anywhere near. Great. Wonderful. I went back to sleep. About five hours later I awoke with the sun and went outside to observe the damage. There, at the site of three makeshift crosses erected in memory of three lives taken in a landslide less than a month before, a group of men and boys had been working all night with shovels, pick axes, and bare hands to clear a path wide enough through the rocks, tree branches, and mud for cars to get past. The first freight truck was about to give it a go. He tried, spit mud and rocks, and when he finally broke through the crowd that had gathered all cheered and we just had now to wait our turn in line.

I made it eventually to Arequipa, rested up a bit and indulged in all the food I couldn't find while on my Machu Picchu trip. The local Peruvian diners serve just about nothing vegetarian, but there is a large movement toward healthy living and various vegetarian restaurants can be found in any city (vegetarians in the small towns are S.O.L.). You can imagine how ecstatic I was to find three of them competing across the street from each other in Lima like gas stations! There is also an abundance of soymilk and soy meat in the market. Vendors there and on the buses bad mouth pharmaceuticals and promote natural alternatives to western medicine that have always worked but are in jeopardy of being erased by the new world order. So I fattened up some in the city and had hoped to see the Colca Canyon while there, but again, due to price gorging and the fact that the canyon was still another six hours away I decided to leave it alone and make my way into Bolivia. Some things are starting to look the same and I don't have the energy or interest to go so far out of my way to see them. My equipment is all falling apart and I'm occupied quite often sewing things back together or looking for replacements. A little tired some days.

I write now from Puno on the north shores of Lake Titicaca. I'll make for the islands of Uros and then across the Bolivian frontier to Copacabana. There's so much more I'd like to write and tell you, but I think I'm pushing my luck with this dangerously long correspondence already, so I'll just wish you all Happy

Holidays with warmth and love and all the best for the New Year.

Love, Dave.

// glittery Christmas lights and people with Santa hats // falafel lunch // mostly wanted a glass of red wine to celebrate // danced like wild monkeys // went to lucha libre today // drank and talked on the church steps // got my wine and weed just like I wanted // to the rhythm of some Andean drummers // taking everything as it comes and just enjoying every minute // new year and I'm still running my head through the same nonsense // got my motor going // karaoke over at the Wild Rover // getting used to not working // tired of waiting // no motivation // sick of dealing with flakes // goddamn hellride // roof started to leak and drip water all over me // all the hotels full // bang on the door, ring the buzzer, and throw rocks at the window for 10 minutes to get back in // reading one of my ruined books // another bus strike // labyrinth of old, blown-out passage ways // weren't allowed to take pictures without paying once over again // talking politics with two lawyers and a truck driver // dogs were chasing me // asked him which way it was to the center. "Center of what?" he asked me // feel really lazy and a little sick // whole eastern half of the country is flooded // 4 bucks for two and a half-days worth of food // there is no hope // nothing lasts very long… just the earth and mountains // made friends with a little white dog and named him "Egypt" // been raining for days // I'll kick someone in the groin if I can't get to the salt flats // in the shower thinking // bathrooms smell like shit and little boys are pissing everywhere // carnival was chaos // everyone in the street is drunk // dying for a good meal // rust beautifully accentuated by the multicolored mountaintops // a little heaven // never ending ever stretching flatness // half rabbit, half chinchilla and bounced like a kangaroo // ripped right through you like a hail of bullets // made a friend at the Chilean customs house //

From: **Paco Paco** (pacogardenrecords@hotmail.com)
Sent: Thu 2/14/08 1:23 AM
To: **All Friends** (amigos@everywhere.com)
Subject: **Bolivia.**

Friends and Family, Brothers and Sisters,

Puno. Lake Titicaca (world's highest lake navigable to large vessels). Not much to see in the town where I left you last but I made my way out into the lake for a visit to the islands of Uros, Amantaní, and Taquile. The Uros are a small group of man made floating islands constructed of reeds piled above the underwater roots of lake plants. Their odd appearance complimented by the colorful dress of their inhabitants and the fairytale-like boats crowned with cartoonish monster heads call to mind the setting of a Tim Burton film. The indigenous who first built the islands did so to distance themselves from invading Europeans and were essentially self-sufficient there, but the site now serves as a tourist stop and the families living there do their best to live off the industry by showing their homes and selling crafts. Farther into the lake I spent the night in the home of a family on the island of Amantaní. A little paradise in the middle of a lake like the sea with no cars, no worries, roaming animals, scattered farms, friendly people, and beautiful views. I slept in a room surrounded by rose bushes near a garden where you can sit in the shade and watch stripes of sunlight scan the bottom of the lake penetrating the crystalline waters while the clouds mix with the mountain tops far off in the distance. A great hail storm passed during the night and I awoke to find little piles of ice in the yard.

I traveled around the southwest coast of the lake to get to Copacabana and there crossed into Bolivia, a country of very diverse landscapes whose soil drank the last blood of such infamous legends as Ernesto "Che" Guevara or Butch Cassidy and the Sundance Kid. A country now plagued by internal conflict, looking for a road to a better future and sick to death of all the political talk-talk with no signs of action. I crawled south from Copacabana and further up into the Andes to Bolivia's capitol, La Paz, where I spent Christmas and New Year's with some Japanese and Brazilian kids I met at the hotel. Christmas was pretty low key, the city lit up from end to end with Christmas lights that faded up into the hills and were lost against the stars. On New Year's Eve we brought out some bottles of champagne, wine, and a whole arsenal of fireworks and ran around the avenues and alleyways shooting rockets at the moon and dancing to the frantic beat of a thousand firecrackers exploding in the streets. La Paz is a fine city full of good food, good nightlife, boundless markets, and is compact enough to walk just about anywhere you'd want to go. I stayed there about three weeks.

Next stop Potosí, the old Spanish colonial mining town said to be the highest city in the world (rivals Lhasa). Here the "Rich Hill," the miners' holy mountain, has been raped for centuries, milked of its goods, barren of its once lucrative silver deposits, but still worked by the sons of sons of miners past who pull what precious metals and minerals they can from its bowels. Touched by neither sun nor moon, toiling away for countless hours beneath the ground, they work their fingers to the bone until enough rock has been cut to quit for the day and they can collect $8-10, if they're lucky. The miners worship and fear the devil god "El Tío" that lives within the mountain. The longer they both please and evade him and manage to stay out of their graves the longer they can put a little food on their family's table and work another day. The miners believe in purity. They believe that in order to coax the mountain and her god out of the best, the purest of their so-desired rocks and minerals that they must be ready to prove themselves and so drink a 96% alcohol, smoke pure black tobacco, chew raw coca leaves, and show no fear to the countless dangers that face them every time they step down into the earth.

On a cold and rainy day in mid-January the miners celebrate their lives, their gods, their profession, their blessings and their curses and, with their tools of trade in hand, dance down from the mines to the plaza in the company of costumed youth and tireless marching bands. They march, sing, dance, and drink to give short lives to their lusts and dreams and for a moment close their eyes to the dirty truth of a hard-dealt life -- an existence as nothing more than mere mortal cogs forgotten in the depths of the great machine. No one would be caught in the parade without a drink in hand and all take their fair share of the miners' special brew. The skies thunder with celebratory TNT charges and a fierce pride shines from the dancers as they're dragged through their movements like marionettes to the pulse of the bass drum and the floating melodies of the brass. Without rest they continue the cleansing ritual, releasing sadness and failure, uplifting goodness and happiness. As the alcohol sets in and the horns begin to slur, the beat loosens and the dancers spin and whirl in the reckless abandon of a ghost dance against gravity. Under the hail of confetti, water balloons, spray foam, and firecrackers they continue until there's no one left to dance.

The Miners' Festival was just a warm up for the big party. By chance I had happened to wander into Bolivia around Carnival time. I didn't know it beforehand, but I'm glad I was there as the city of Oruro hosts one of the most famous and festive carnivals in South America. A parade of wonderfully costumed dancers that tells the history of Bolivia... of its workers, it's African slaves, of its land and its religious adaptations and cultural heritage. "La Diablada," (devil dance) a non-stop celebration and show of imaginative, creative, and weird creatures blending into a wild wave of movement, driven by an army of drums and horns seething through the crowded streets, greeted and cheered upon by thousands of spectators who line the sidewalks and wage water balloon wars against each other during the parade gaps. The procession wiggles its way through town; all the devils, bears, and weirdoes chased by Saint Michael the Archangel and a multitude of traditional dancers from all sides of the country. The costumes are the pride of the festival. Meticulously decorated from bottom to top with mirrors, chains, sparkles, stripes, sequins, capes, boots, extravagant masks with bulging eyes and gnashing teeth, fur, claws, bells, whistles, and noisemakers of all shapes and sizes. Songs, cheers, and chants accompany the dances and are echoed back to the marchers by the enthusiastic crowd that surrounds them. By nightfall the party and parade in the streets haven't lessened any, but the interest of many of the drinkers has deteriorated into brawls and catcalls. The streets all smell like piss and there are piles of garbage on every corner. Music from the marching bands continues into the wee hours of the morning but is rivaled by the bass boom erupting from downtown dance clubs. When Monday rolls around and the official festivities of the long weekend are over most folks are relaxing, recovering, or on their way out of town but the few who have still to get the party out of their systems run around the streets armed with spray foam, water guns, and a few instruments, drums, and costumes and carry on the nonsense and chaos until they drop from exhaustion.

Getting out of Oruro after Carnival was a chore. With more than 30, 000 extra folks in town the transports filled up fast. I finally caught a night bus out on the rocky road to Uyuni, the jump off point for crossing the south desert into Chile. With a caravan of jeeps we set off on a 3-day 4WD adventure that would take us through barren, dreamlike landscapes all but forgotten and untouched except where our sturdy, studded tires cut serpentine-like trails into the sand and rock and left behind them swirling clouds of dust dissipating into the wind. We passed the train cemetery where lie rusting away some of the first narrow gauge railway locomotives of South America. We passed the Uyuni salt flats, a surreal stretch of infinite white plane now covered with a thin layer of water mirroring the heavens and creating the illusion of endless sky through which float little people taking pictures and our jeeps, Siamese-twinned and split down the middle by a Rorschach spray of water. The Valley of the Rocks is a garden of misshapen, windblown, twisted, and mutilated natural stone sculptures that appear as gargoyles or vultures perched high above the road waiting eternally for passing prey or like frozen, sleeping giants... stoic and immobile guardians of an ancient arid valley. Ages of volcanic activity have stained the soil in a wash of varied colors accentuated by the snow-capped peaks, small green shrubbery, and the brave and cloudless blue sky. In the south desert remain many lagoons tainted by strong mineral presence or communities of micro-organisms which give them new and strange faces... a green lagoon, a red lagoon, a turquoise and white lagoon full of radiant pink flamingos that sits at the base of a crippled old volcano built up of burnt red rock, edged in a charred black dust spit and sprayed by a violent and unchallenged wind. We passed wild and wandering herds of hairy llama and their long neck cousin, the vicuña. We passed a field of bubbling, hazy geysers and at five thousand meters above sea level stopped for a sunrise swim in a natural hot spring that flows into a steamy, swampy prehistoric lake.

I said my goodbyes to Bolivia at a lonely customs house on the beaten desert road in the middle of nowhere and caught a transport down the steep incline (a quick drop of 2500 m) to the pleasant bohemian village of San Pedro de Atacama, Chile -- very reminiscent of Santa Fe, New Mexico. Actually, I write now from the capitol, Santiago, and I've felt very comfortable here. Very like Southern California... very familiar... very strange... I'm falling fast towards the south and should hit Tierra del Fuego within the next few weeks. Hope you all are well and warm.

Love, Dave.

From: **Paco Paco** (pacogardenrecords@hotmail.com)
Sent: Fri 2/29/08 6:32 PM
To: **All Friends** (amigos@everywhere.com)
Subject: **Thoughts from the End of the Earth.**

Friends and Family, Brothers and Sisters…

I made it. Ushuai, Tierra del Fuego. End of the line. A year and a half ago I set out from Los Angeles on a southbound descent over land to the final point of the Americas. End of the world. Here I am just eight hundred miles shy of Antarctica and what a journey it's been. Mexico, Central America, and so far the western half of South America. It's been a journey of learning. A session of classes in the great school of life. I've seen a lot of places and come to know a good many beautiful people. To report to you as I have so many times before that the inhabitants of the countries through which I've passed have been "so friendly, so kind" may eventually grow repetitive or lose its sense of meaning, but in truth I've been brought to my knees time and again by the blind generosity and humble, unyielding hospitality I've found in the homes and peoples I've met along the way.

So many faces, so many colors, so many open hearts, truthful eyes and welcoming hands. So many ideas, so many little fires burning in ready minds. My travels have shown me that we all drink from the same cup of life whose blood flows in rivers and streams to all ends of the earth and through this we are all united. Through the common breath we draw we enter into a brotherhood of spirits and it doesn't matter where in the world we live, how we communicate, or to what gods we offer up our prayers because in the end as we go spinning around on this ball of rock together, wrestling to gain a little piece of happiness from our individual battles and hardships (from which no one is exempt), all those minor differences blur and we blend into one people who will either sink or swim collectively depending on how much effort we devote to understanding and, in effect, respecting each other as equal beings blessed with that little spark of electricity and soul which allows us to breath and to live. To exist.

Life is beautiful. Life is a flower. But I see also that in our blood a sickness breeds. A disease that urges us to separate ourselves and reinforce our borders. A worm that probes for the weaknesses that lie between us, so easy to exploit, so easy to further divide us, blind us, and numb us to the magic, majestic life that flows in and around us. A life with the capacity to provide for everyone it touches but for when by our own hands we choke it, pollute it, and abuse it to the point where we no longer recognize it in the environment in which we live or the faces of our brothers and sisters, mothers, fathers, sons and daughters with whom we share it every day.

Evolution travels in a slow bus. But it seems to me that by now, in 2008, we should be organizing ourselves to move forward towards a better human and universal understanding. We ought to be looking for ways to more efficiently educate and elevate ourselves and our children, rather than to distance and distract ourselves from the wondrous beauty that inspires our lives, cultures, colors and thoughts.

Times are changing. We are growing. From the dying flames of ignorance and apathy we will rise in a new war dance of liberation. A dance to shake off the oppression we inflict on ourselves and our own minds when we ignore the patient bleating of our hearts and the vision of our own humanity reflected in the eyes of those with whom we share the pulse.

We dance that our civilization shall be measured not by our manner of dress, nor by the grandeur of the buildings we erect, not even by the advances in our technology, but in the quality of treatment we extend towards one another and our earth. The future will be shaped by the lengths at which we strive to ensure that everyone receives (or has the means to) the education, exposure, and experience that ultimately delivers us all.

Travel has taught me that survival depends on education and experience. The experiences that shape our lives are the same that we use to weigh our decisions, and we live by the decisions we make. We elect to move forward in life or sit idly by in decay. We choose to be or not to. How we treat ourselves and our brethren is up to us. Things change only by our actions, and I understand now that the revolution we seek is really just the evolution of our thought process; that a call to arms is truly a cry to embrace our beauties and differences. As the stripes of a rainbow celebrate each other's company, so we know that without each other we don't amount to much.

We live in a world based on borders, fenced and divided, partly ignored, where our fears and illusions are fed by the lack of contact with those whom we have yet to meet. Talk to strangers. Stay out late. We need to tear down the walls that separate or confine us. Those old, battered bricks can be used to build up a stronger foundation of human understanding, one that can support our colors and cultures and allow us room to expand our global knowledge, free from the threat and encroachment of ignorance, greed, and all these divisions slicing at our wrists, imprisoning our minds, and strangling our ability to love and to live. I've seen that peace can live in the hearts of men, but it must be taught, learned, and nurtured. Those who have the keys must unlock the doors. The responsibility lies with us all.

Now that I've run out of land to the south I guess I'll turn around and head back up north. Argentina and Brazil await!

Love, Dave.

// the 24 hours on the bus weren't so bad // pre-made peyote // eating cherries // I want to punch someone // selling veggie burgers on the street corner // three days with pure tourists // thick mist clinging to the ground // spent a night on the open sea // great gales blasting from the southeast // easiest in life to just go with the flow // my knees would never go for it // waited about 3 hours and only got a ride about 2 kilometers // end of the line // good god… looking at the map now and I don't want to go back up // bored of the bullshit // internet connections in Patagonia are shit // first pine cones // stamp that says I've been to the end of the world // clean, fine breeze… not too many people // light blue, dark blue, crystalline // packed to the gills with globe trotters and digital cameras // walked and walked and walked and walked // footprints I'd been following // not much else but skeletons and dust // gave me some bread and jelly // woke up early and made a fire // motorcycle came around the bend and said he could take one of us // beautiful day today // sweet forest of bamboo // where will I be tomorrow? // burning through money // weird but kinda cool outdoor art // back to basics // rose bushes, ponds, bridges // don't feel like anything's changed // up on the roof looking out over the city // played some race car games at the arcade // actually said, "Let me put on something a little more comfortable." // musicians sure could play // I'm split, like always // just hovering on the surface // a city's a city and I've seen a few // I don't know about all that // April Fool's Day // a forever burning flame // with a group of kids from Paraguay // malnutrition and lack of strenuous exercise //

From: **Paco Paco** (pacogardenrecords@hotmail.com)
Sent: Sun 3/30/08 9:55 PM
To: **All Friends** (amigos@everywhere.com)
Subject: **Patagonia.**

Friends and Family, Brothers and Sisters…

Patagonia. Not so many people. A vast expanse of mainly untouched lands, barren, wind-torn deserts, impenetrable rocky mountains, massive rivers of ice, thick forest, tundra, expansive lakes, and extreme winters. Patagonia, so named by Magellan when, on his arrival, he encountered a very giant people and is rumored to have said, "My, what big feet you have!" The Spanish "patagonia" means "land of the big feet."

With a couple of beach breaks in the north of Chile and a quick tour of Santiago I set off for Puerto Montt where I would catch a three-day ferry boat through the channels of western Patagonia to the southern port of Natales. As I neared Puerto Montt I was excited to see a great change in the atmosphere. We began to enter thick pine that cut into the watery skies and triangular wood homes painted in warm tones began to pop up all around. I boarded my old Japanese ferry for the trip south along with tons of cargo, autos, and other passengers. Late in the evening we disembarked from Puerto Montt into the long network of islands and waterways that comprise the southern coast of Chile.

The sun made very few appearances as we pushed on through a ghostly white mist in pure silence aside from the low hum and rhythmic percussion of the engine and the lively chitchat of passengers keeping warm inside. The crew guided the boat through many very narrow passages and in those wider we were entertained by playful visits from curious dolphins and sea otters. Someone claimed to have seen a whale. On the third day we were hit by a furious storm whose gales, as if blown straight from the lungs of Neptune himself, kept the huge ferry floating at an angle as it stood against their assault. We were enclosed in a constant drizzle and every so often a blast of cold wind shot down the channel sending rain like a spray of stray bullets smashing against the glass windows and weathered metal walls of the ship. The storm died out as we neared our destination and I spent a few rainless days there hiking with friends in the stunningly intriguing Torres del Paine National Park before continuing on to Punta Arenas and Tierra del Fuego by land.

Tierra del Fuego... The island province detached from South America by the Strait of Magellan and divided politically between Chile and Argentina, where the great Andes mountain range (that I'd been traveling along since Colombia) finally sinks in into the sea. Where the Atlantic and Pacific Oceans meet in a cold collision of wild waters that have devastated explorers and sailors for centuries. Tierra del Fuego, the "Land of Fire," so named by Magellan (again) who observed from a distance the many campfires of the island natives burning deep in the night. After a year and a half on the road I finally made it to my destination, just 800 miles shy of Antarctica where the sign at the entrance to the small town of Ushuaia reads, "Welcome to the End of the World." I'm not sure what I expected to find in the south of the south. It looks a lot like I would imagine northern Canada or Alaska to appear. Very beautiful. Calm. Almost undisturbed. I arrived as the southern hemisphere's summer was on the way out the door and there was no snow to be found aside from that which resides always up in the mountains. A very spring like weather made the days pleasant to wander. The town of Ushuaia is pretty enough to walk around but in terms of tourist attractions is just a playground for big bucks, so I did a couple mountain hikes, threw a rock at Antarctica, and turned around to head back north.

Eastern Patagonia consists of a vast desert plain, but I kept to the west and the wooded hills where sits the Glaciers National Park, home to the famous Perito Moreno Glacier, one of the world's only advancing ice fields. This monster is part of an ice camp that takes up more area than the city of Buenos Aires (a city of some twelve million inhabitants) and is about as tall as a twenty story-building top to bottom, with a face that stretches some five kilometers across. When chunks of ice the size of small houses break off and slam into the water below the roar can be heard for miles. To the north of the Moreno Glacier lies the intimidating Mount Fitz Roy and its companions just outside the quiet little town of El Chaltén. Here young, jagged, shark-toothed mountains born of a continental crash rise sharply, brazenly from the plains, silhouetted in the evening by abrasive, vibrant sunsets that explode across the sky.

The crevasses of these mountains' black ridges are frozen solid with an ice that never melts and the trees that grow down below are forever crooked, bent, and twisted as a result of ongoing exposure to an unchecked wind... a fierce and driving wind that can knock you down. It forces you to put all your weight in front of you and to really lean into it to keep from being blown backwards, so much so that when the wind decides to change direction or abruptly die down, you nearly tumble face forward into the dirt. Ice particles suspended in the frigid waters that flow down from the high slopes color the streams and rivers turquoise, opaque and obscure hues.

I left the Glaciers park without seeing as much as I would have liked to on account of my knees being about worn out from over-use and made a refreshing and lazy visit to the lakes and lagoons of Bariloche, the chocolate capitol, which I found to be very reminiscent of Colorado, except that the streets are filled with sweets and that tempting, hedonistic atmosphere gives it something of a Willy Wonka twist.

Back on the road I got lost in the desert looking for the prehistoric "Cave of the Hands" in which an ancient tribe left colorful wall paintings of themselves, the animals they hunted, rituals, and, of course, hands. Hundreds of hands, they say. I don't know first 'hand' because I never made it. I took a wrong turn somewhere and got worried when I found myself in a valley devoid of human footprints surrounded by sun-bleached animal skeletons and rotting carcasses without water, food, or shelter, at least a four-hour walk from the highway with dusk setting on. I left and didn't care to attempt the five-plus-hour walk all over again the following day.

Instead, I cut back to the coast and to the Peninsula Valdez nature reserve. The killer whales here are known to rush out of the water and snatch baby sea lions off the beach as a midday snack. I watched an orca's fin circle in the shallows very close but it never left the water. I did see a ton of cute little baby sea lions, of course, as well as big sea elephants, an army of penguins, armadillo, fox, ostrich, and llama-like guanaco.

I write now from the pumping cosmopolitan capitol of Buenos Aires. The immense and enigmatic city is worlds away from any other I've seen on my trip (excluding maybe Mexico City) and I fell in love with it instantly. Full of a little bit of anything you could ever want (except, of course, diversified food outlets) available twenty-four hours a day. Tango, discos, music in the street, arts, plazas, cheap subway, way too many statues, crowds of people, insanity, creativity, energy, lots of spots to hang out and be lazy, things new and strange, things old and familiar, crime, friendship, bureaucracy, sprawling sky scrapers, lights, sights, graffiti, and a whole lot of traffic. What impresses me most, though, in Buenos Aires are the buildings. Old, grand, classical masterpieces strewn throughout the city. A lot of art nouveau, as well, from the early twentieth century. My friend Robyn came all the way from California for a visit and we ran around town causing trouble for a few days. I also crossed paths and spent some time with a few other travel-happy amigos I'd met along the way.

Buenos Aires would be a city I could get comfortable in, but I want to keep moving for the time being. I feel a little lost now that my initial mission is complete... like the anchor that had been pulling me forever south has been cut and I'm wandering now without direction or destination. I have my mind on a couple other trips I'd like to do, but for now I'll keep heading north. Off to Brazil!

Until next time...

Love, Dave.

// today was a fucking mental mess // bummer being poor // able to do so much on so little for so long // falls were dazzling // battered mists carried off by the breeze // butterflies that landed all over me // have a black mark on my conscience // idiots using the bathroom to do cocaine // little respect for much but their own selfish desires // snoring bastard in my room // fine sun-touched feminine creatures // the only thing that counts // go back to the boulders today and dive off of them // just have to walk with the faith that I won't // find a new way // millions of windows encircle you with secret spies inside // pulsing with a tense and surging unrest // visa situation in Venezuela // ghost town like Sunday // 20 days left in Brazil // missed the fucking bus // cheap plate of yakisoba and french fries // elevated energy in the streets // still have a long way to go // with a soul and a smile // fucking tiger // in more boring news // tomorrow to the beach // slave trade and the resulting culture and religion // watched some more capoeria in the plaza // found a quiet little spot on the coast // ricochet echo of sporadic African drums shattering throughout the streets // way out of this problem of poverty // kept me on the level // mouth of the Amazon // earth turning darker // little exotic birds // a while to relax // sky washed in pale and deep blues // just like little pirates // feeling fine // got scolded for hanging my hammock // everywhere trash // dead west into the sun // the spiders were having a feast // the water silver, like a mirror // either he's a big story teller or he has an interesting story to tell // replaced by the roar of howler monkeys // tinted like tea from all the fallen leaves // traveling makes my brain hurt // drizzly when I arrived // falling apart quickly // dark and "dangerous" streets of Caracas // tasty vegetarian meal // brought about memories // maybe I'll always roam. Float like a piece of driftwood on a long, long river. That could be alright. I could get used to it, I guess //

From: **Paco Paco** (pacogardenrecords@hotmail.com)
Sent: Fri 5/16/08 6:33 PM
To: **All Friends** (amigos@everywhere.com)
Subject: **Brazil and Back.**

Friends and Family, Brothers and Sisters…

I'm on the way back to the States. Writing you
now from the Finca Tatin in Guatemala. Hanging out
here in the summer heat for a bit. Stopped off to see old
friends, relax and recollect myself before crashing once
again into the rat race up north. My travel battery finally
burned out. I felt it go back in Buenos Aires. Like a
rubber band it snapped and I realized I wasn't enjoying
being Joe Tourist anymore… taking pictures everyday,
changing money, getting lost, battling self-imposed
poverty, tired, dirty and hungry, searching for
something to put in my belly … it was all starting to get
unpleasantly repetitive and the cities and sites were
beginning to look the same. I love to travel and see new
things so I knew it must just be that this trip was
reaching its end. Time for a break. Time to work and
pass the days with familiar faces. With my funds
quickly disappearing as well as my patience I decided to
cut back north and spend the summer working,
motorcycling, BBQing, or employing myself in some
other equally important pastime. Something old and
familiar will once again be refreshing and fun.

I arrived in Guatemala on a flight from
Caracas, Venezuela, about a week ago but first had to
pass through the great southern empire of Brazil -- a

country known as "The Continent" due to both its size and linguistic/geographic isolation: one of the only non-Spanish speaking countries in Latin America and cut off from many of its neighbors by the Andes mountain range and Amazon swamps. Despite this isolation Brazil has managed to keep its name on the lips of the world. Tales of the Amazon Basin and its extensive rain forests and wildlife are well known throughout the globe. So too, of course, are the infamous Rio Carnival and much-fantasized Brazilian beaches lined with drop-dead gorgeous girls, muscle beach men, white sands, coconut groves, and dolphins gliding playfully in and out of the water in front of gloriously painted sunset skies. It's all there, I assure you. All that and more, although maybe not quite as fantastic as you might have envisioned. After all they're just people and cities like everywhere else. The Discovery Channel could definitely give you a better report on Brazil than I, but I'll tell you a little bit about what I saw.

From Buenos Aires I climbed north a few hours to Rosario, birthplace of the revolutionary Ernesto "Che" Guevara, who is arguably more popular in South America than Jesus Christ. From there I caught an almost empty night bus up to Iguazú Falls, the spectacular series of cascades and crushing waterfalls that tumble over the border into Brazil. The falls had been on my list of things to do from the get go and I was excited to be there, however slightly less so when they charged me $150 for a thirty-day visa to enter the country. Not being financially prepared to spend more than thirty days there anyway, I went on in to see what I could. Brazil is a big chunk of land. Lots to see. Far too much for just one month on a strict budget. Iguazú is actually more stimulating from the Argentine side. The flat and lazy river that saunters through the outer Amazon plain suddenly drops over a cliff delivering tons of water crashing down onto the rocks and pools below. A waterfall is one thing, a pretty thing at that, but to see so many together at once in so many forms, faces, and levels of force framed by a palm tree paradise full of wild little creatures is something else entirely. It's like a theme park. An elevated metal walkway takes you up over the falls and down into the rainforest where the big cat-sized bear/raccoon-like 'coatís' aren't afraid to help themselves to a look at what snacks you've brought in your pocket. Monkeys sing through the trees and the signs along the path warn of venomous biting things that live beneath the leaves. Great fun!

From Iguazú I jumped over to Florianopolis, the southern island city on the sea blessed with pristine beaches in sufficient quantity such as you can easily find a quiet spot to yourself. I then made great leaps and bounds up the coast in devastatingly long bus trips, stopping off at key cities like Sao Paolo, the rushing and raging metropolis where the weathered buildings rise to the sky, tattooed to the top in gang insignia indecipherable to the layman eye like an extraterrestrial code left to ruin on an abandoned ship. The city is hot. There's a heat in the streets. A kind of uneasy energy or critical unrest. Next stop, Rio de Janeiro, the gem of the Brazilian metropolis nestled between lush green hills hewn together by lengthy beaches against which lap the warm blue waters of the Atlantic Ocean. Buddy Christ looks out over the bay and the shantytown favelas cling to the hills at its sides. Copacabana and Impanema are packed to the gills on the weekends and people-watching is a popular sport. Up to Salvador de Bahia where the streets shake to the rolling rhythm of African drums whose echoes beat out through the cobblestone alleyways and into the night where thick, rich Creole food is served by heavyset, dark-skinned women in long white gowns and colorful headdress.

And on into the jungle of jungles. I caught a riverboat in Belém that would take me five days upstream on the great flood of water they call the Amazon River. I expected something big. I've seen the Discovery Channel. I knew a lot of water moved through those banks. But none of that prepared me for the true grand immensity that this so-called "river" conveys. I felt, rather, that I was crossing a huge lake or sea. I squinted and strained at times to see the other side. We passed gigantic islands, cities, fishing villages, freight barges, oil tankers, and on and on... The Amazon River is big. Really big.

The roof beams of the ferry were equipped with hooks for the passengers to hang up their hammocks. First ones on board got the best spots for the long journey but before long the crowds came in and I found myself squeezing into my hammock through other peoples shoulders, elbows, or feet. Cozy. The night we left from Belém the entire interior of the ship was converted into a multi-colored web of crisscrossed suspended sleepers. At first I wasn't sure I could spend five days on a boat full of people who seemed to think the best place for their garbage was in the river, no matter if they had to stand in front of a trash can to throw it overboard. I got to thinking, though, "Well, what do we do with our trash? Bury it in a landfill? Unseen, unheard? What's the difference in the end?" It would seem more important that we educate more and consume less, at least less plastics and "packaging," and help to support effective recycling programs worldwide. So my shipmates, although perhaps miseducated, weren't so bad. We played cards, struggled to converse in Portuguese, and sat around sun tanning on the deck admiring the view to pass the time.

At the end of the fifth day we arrived in Manaus and I met up with a few guys who were going into the jungle for some days. How could I not go? By manner of boats, trucks, taxis, and canoes we made our way into the backwaters and arrived at the home of a local family along the Ariau River who would put us up for the next few nights. Edison, the father, was a real jungle know-it-all and took us all over to see crocodiles, tree sloths, monkeys, pink and gray dolphins, hidden rivers, rainbow-colored fish, many medicinal plants, and fantastic new fruits. At one point I had one strange, new, and delicious fruit falling apart in the right hand, a different but equally delightful one in a similar state in the left, and something wonderfully sweet and sticky smeared all over my face. Happiness.

The Amazon was great and Edison's family very hospitable but it all made me miss my jungle life back in Guatemala so when we returned to Manaus I hopped on a bus up through Venezuela to Caracas where I thought I was getting a good flight deal. But the bus was more expensive than I expected and I was less than pleased at the airport when informed that I would need to pay almost $100 in international airport tax (above the other taxes I'd already paid with the ticket) to leave the country. However, I paid my dues to organized crime, caught my plane, and now I'm here and all's well.

Seems strange to be in Guatemala now. Not much has changed. In many ways I feel like I never left. Like South America was just a hazy dream from a few nights ago as I'm sure the entire adventure will become as soon as I fall back into the rhythm of North American life. To tell the truth, I'm a little hesitant to hang up my gypsy boots. I've grown quite comfortable in them. I have some reservations about settling into a real job and taking up an apartment, but I think there's something to be said for having a little bit of stability as well. A place to call your own … at least for a while.

Until next time…

Love, Dave.

124

A collection of photographs taken by Dave Paco during this adventure can be seen on our Facebook page:
www.facebook.com/pacogarden
...Look in the "Walk" folder.

61996540R00076

Made in the USA
Lexington, KY
26 March 2017